AF394442

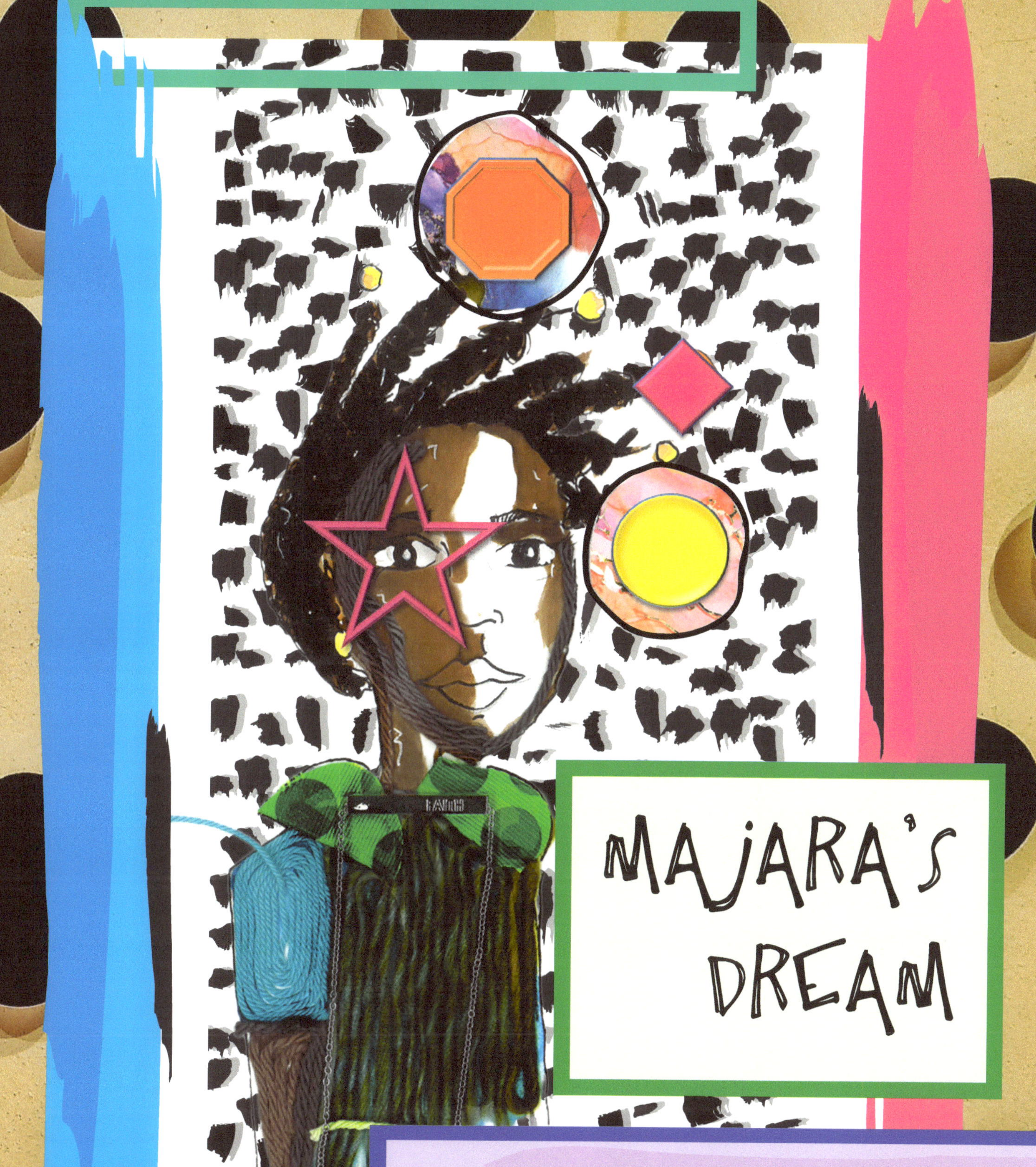

MAJARA'S DREAM
WRITTEN AND ILLUSTRATED BY
MARCI RODGERS

I dedicate this book to my father,
my mother and my sister.
I love you.

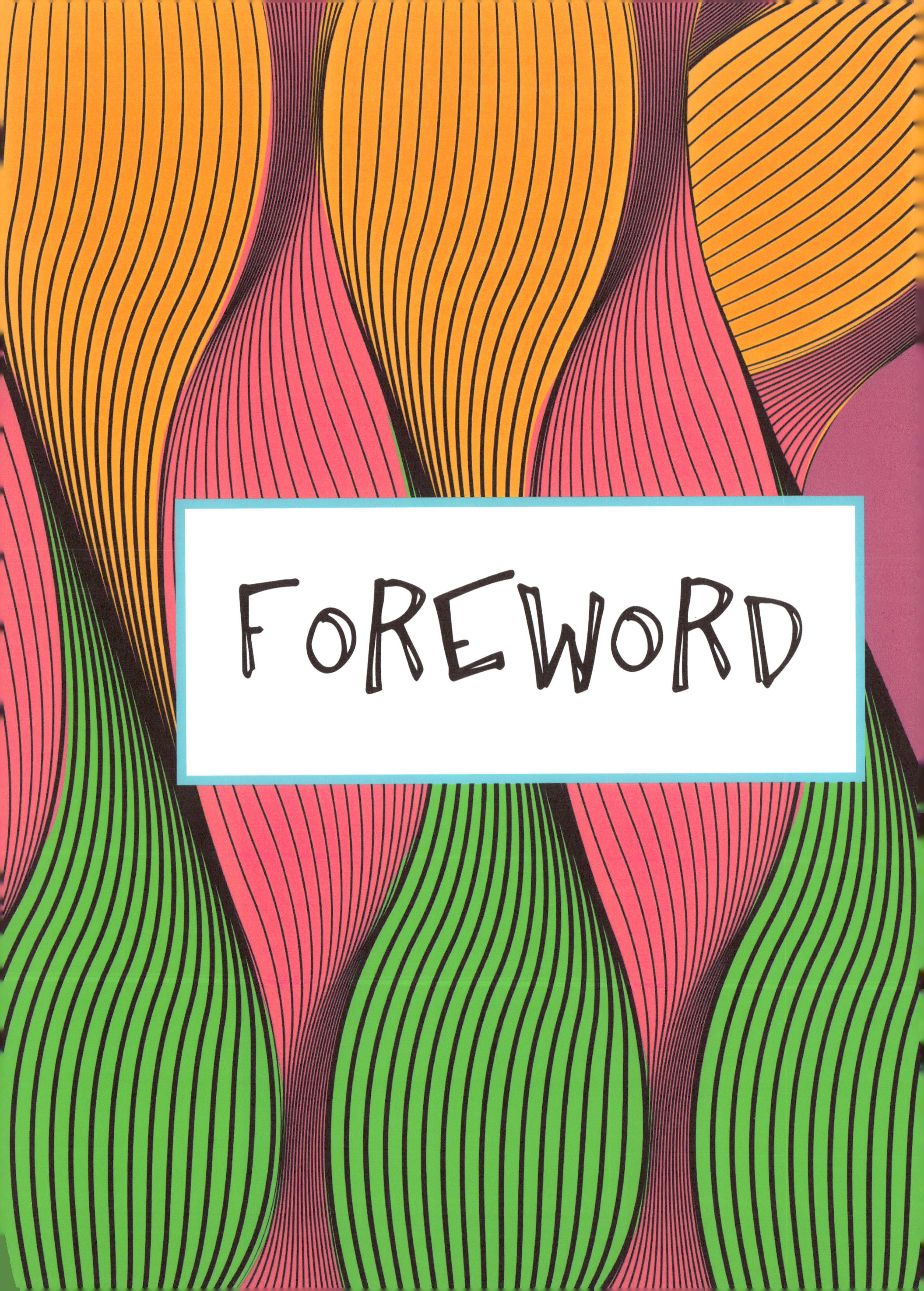
FOREWORD

BEFORE YOU TURN THE PAGE, I MUST GIVE
A DISCLAIMER. THIS IS NOT YOUR "TRADITIONAL"
CHILDREN'S BOOK.

IT IS HOWEVER A TOOL FOR INSPIRATION.

THE INTENDED FORMATTING OF THE FOLLOWING TEXT
IS TO BE SOLELY USED AS A FRAME OF REFERENCE
AND GUIDE TO THE BELIEVER, SEEKER AND MOST
OF
ALL THE DREAMER. MY HOPE IS THE DREAMER
WHO DECIDES TO PARTAKE IN THIS TEXT/WORKBOOK
CONTINUES TO DREAM FOR US ALL. HUMANITY IS IN
NEED OF ART AND LOVE.

THANK YOU IN ADVANCE FOR YOUR UNDERSTANDING
AND FOR SEEING THE WORLD THROUGH
MAJARA'S EYES.

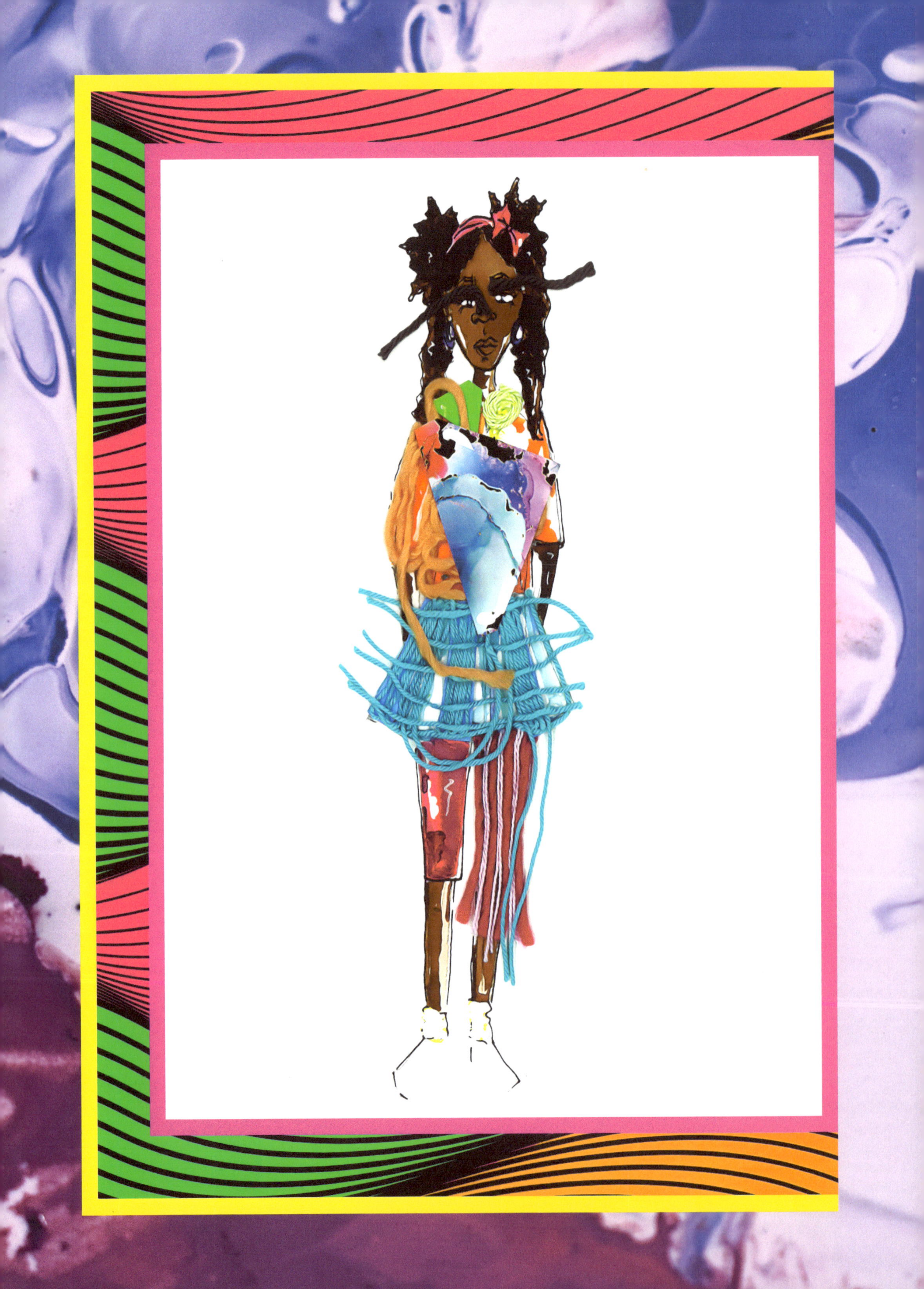

HELLO!

I AM MAJARA (MAH-JAH-RAA). I LOVE ART AND I AM LUCKY ENOUGH THAT ART IS MY JOB. I DESIGN COSTUMES FOR THEATERS AND FAMOUS ACTORS. DESIGNING COSTUMES FOR THEATRE AND FAMOUS ACTORS IS MY FAVORITE FORM OF ART.

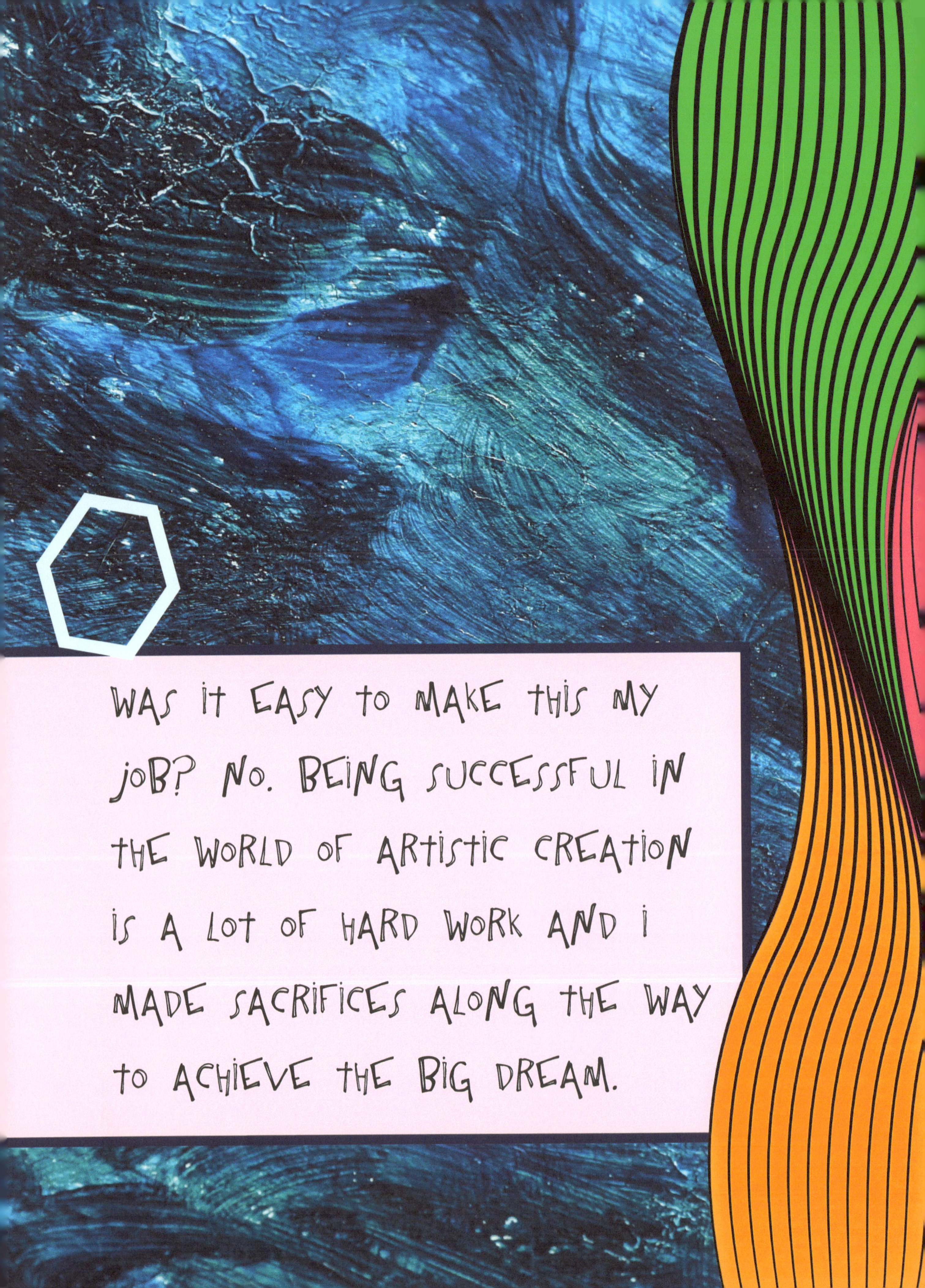
WAS IT EASY TO MAKE THIS MY JOB? NO. BEING SUCCESSFUL IN THE WORLD OF ARTISTIC CREATION IS A LOT OF HARD WORK AND I MADE SACRIFICES ALONG THE WAY TO ACHIEVE THE BIG DREAM.

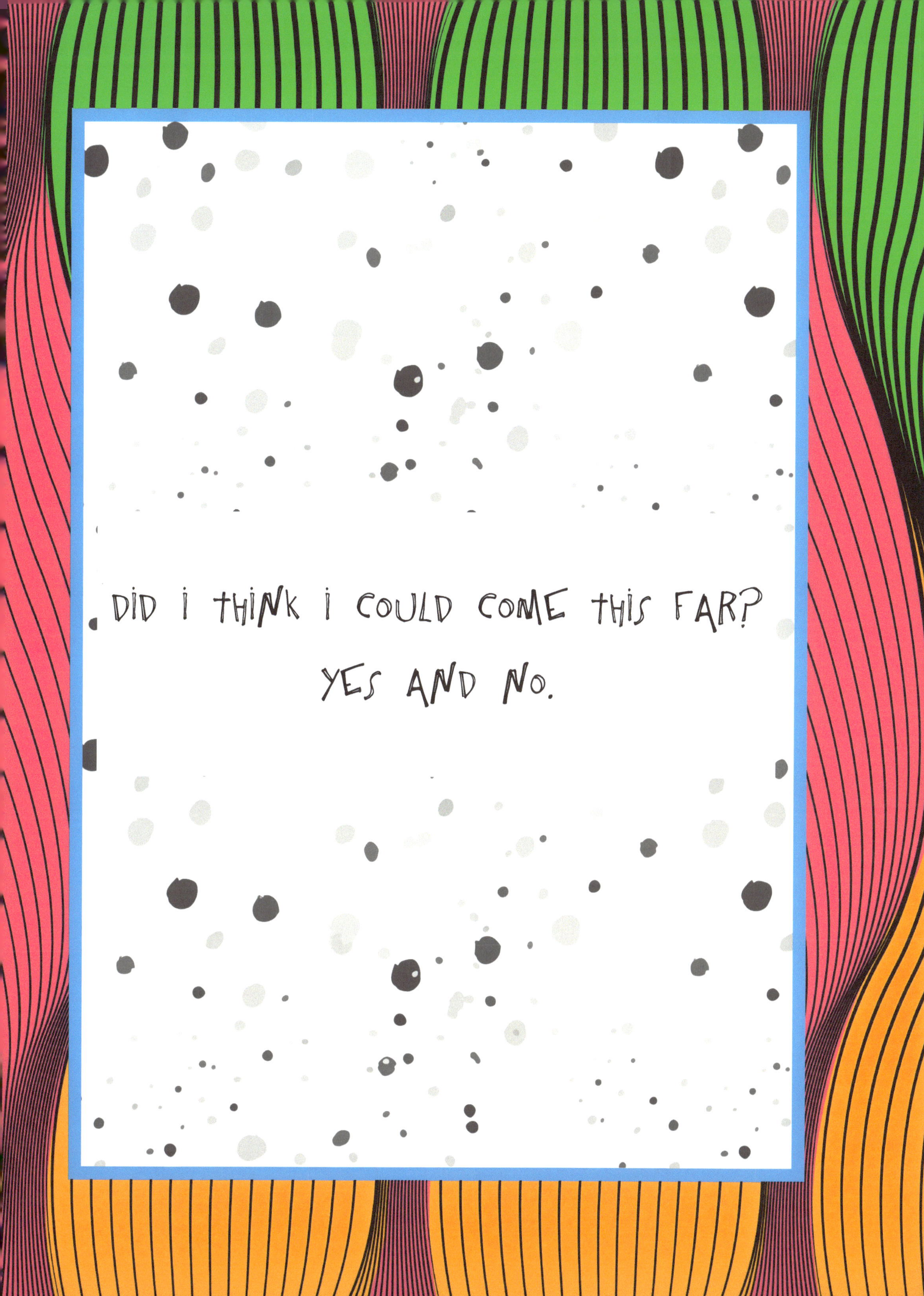
DID I THINK I COULD COME THIS FAR?
YES AND NO.

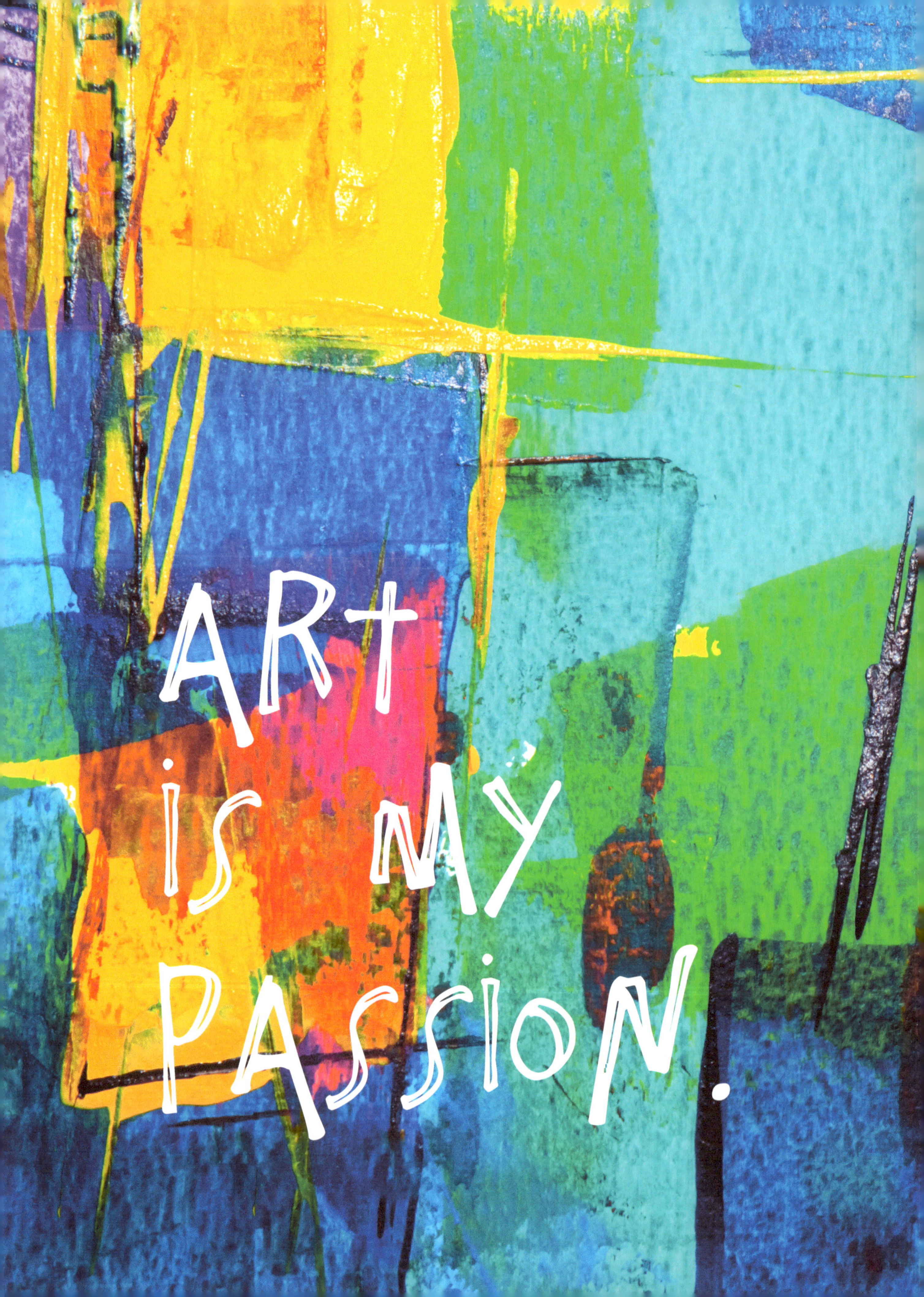
ARt
is my
PASSioN.

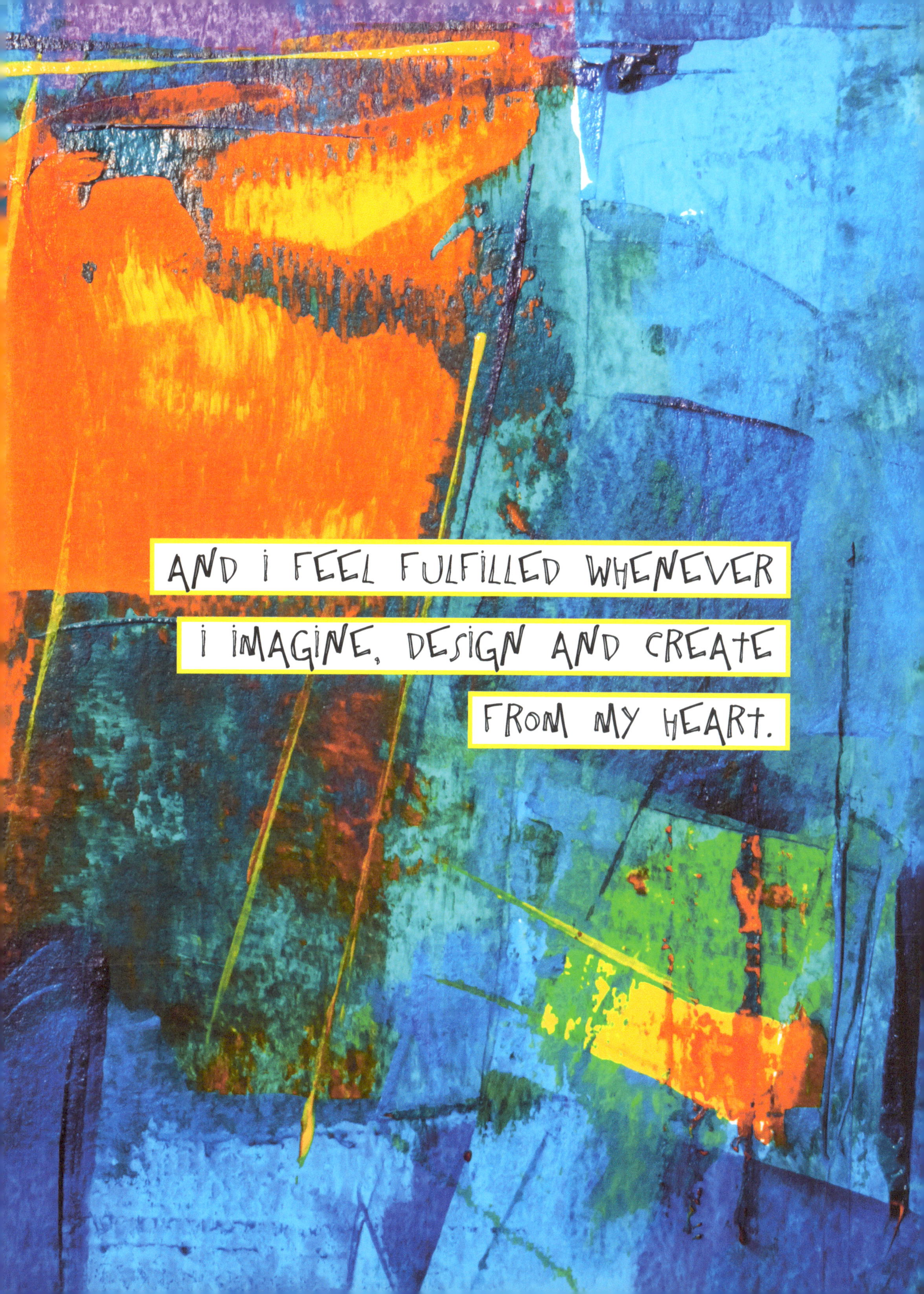
AND I FEEL FULFILLED WHENEVER
I IMAGINE, DESIGN AND CREATE
FROM MY HEART.

SOMETIMES, IT WAS HARD
TO HOLD ONTO A DREAM
THIS BIG; BUT MY MOTHER
ALWAYS TOLD ME,

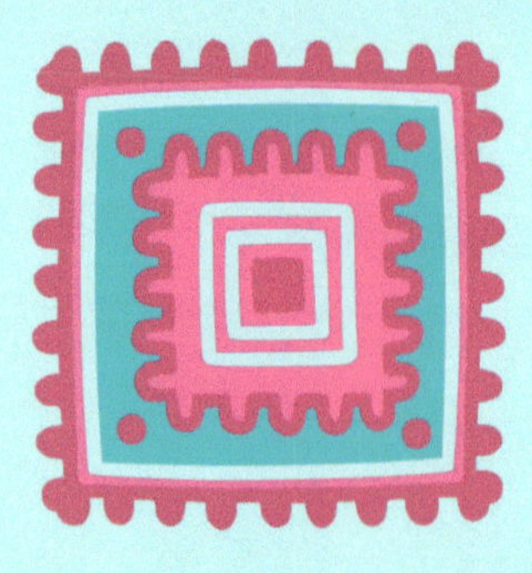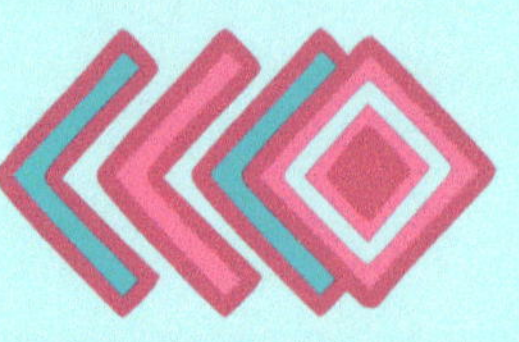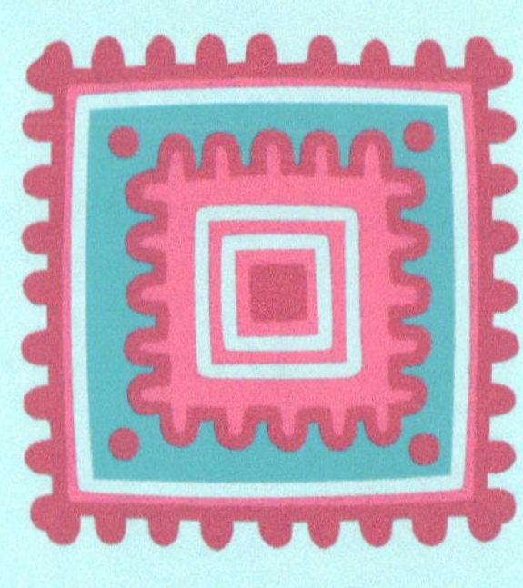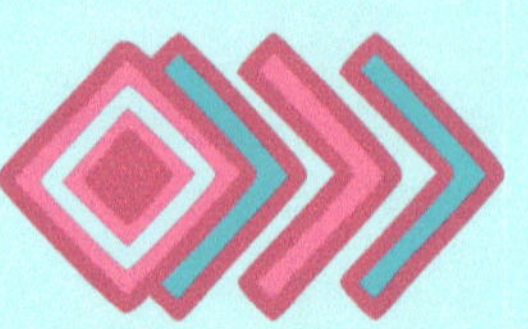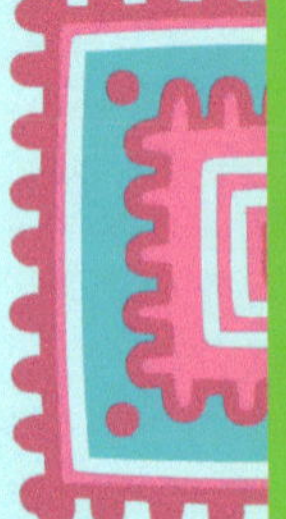

"TO BE MYSELF
AND HAVE FAITH".

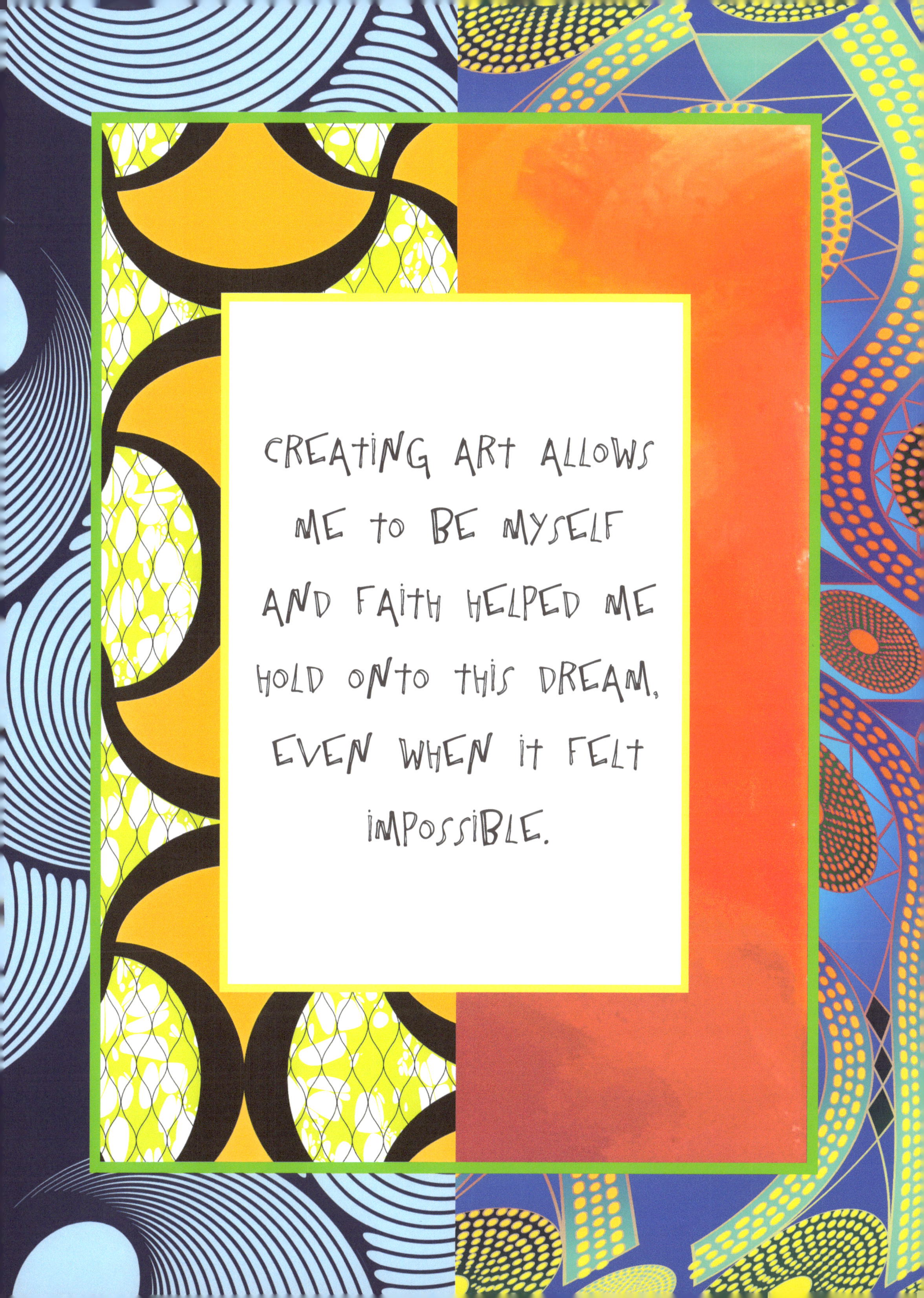

CREATING ART ALLOWS ME TO BE MYSELF AND FAITH HELPED ME HOLD ONTO THIS DREAM, EVEN WHEN IT FELT IMPOSSIBLE.

WAS IT ALL WORTH IT?

YES!
NOTHING CAN TAKE AWAY
THE SKILLS I HAVE LEARNED.
NOTHING CAN STOP MY
IMAGINATION FROM FLOWING
THROUGH MY FINGERTIPS, AND
NOTHING CAN HOLD ME BACK
FROM PUTTING IN HARD WORK,
FOR MY BIG DREAM.

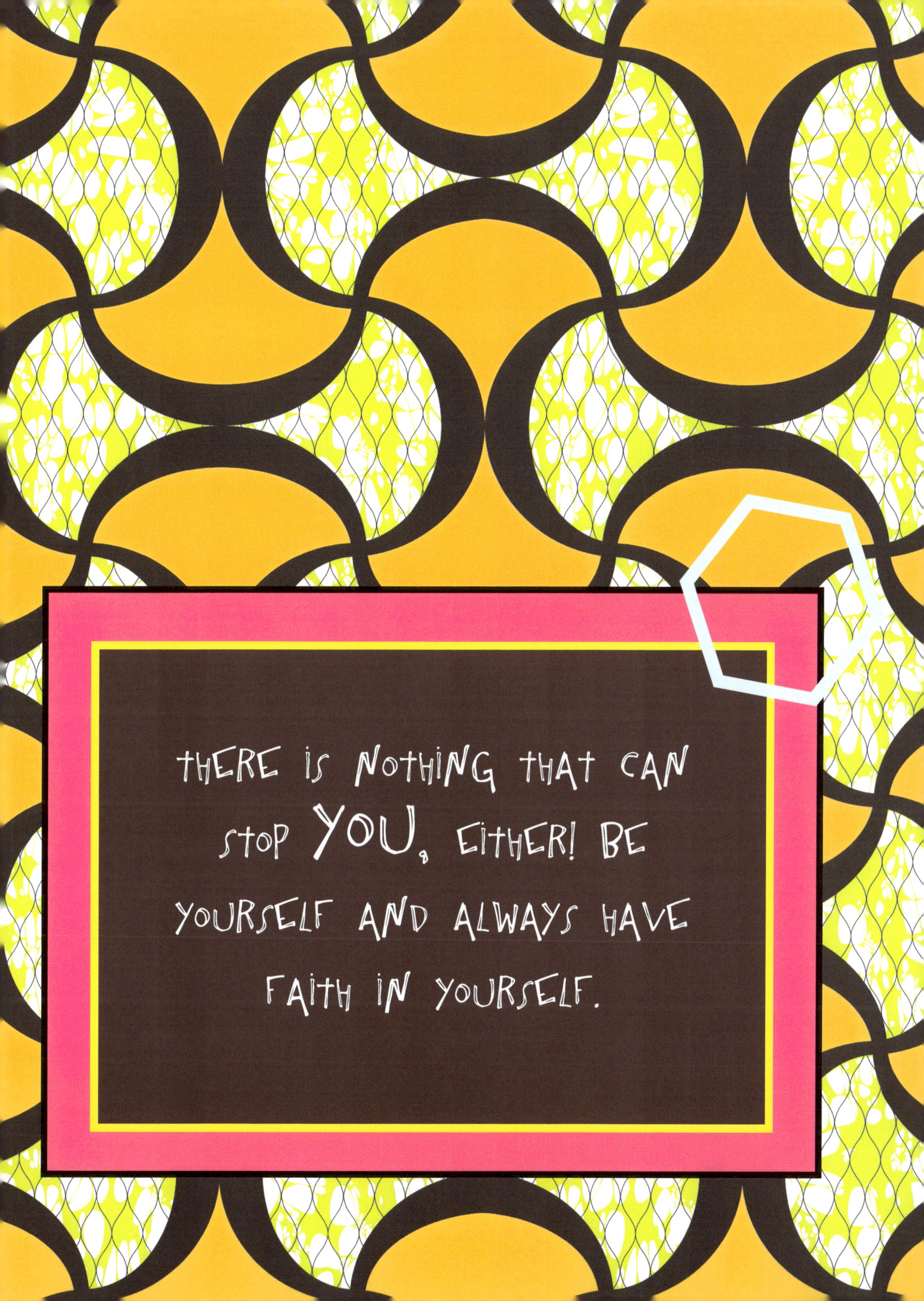
THERE IS NOTHING THAT CAN STOP YOU, EITHER! BE YOURSELF AND ALWAYS HAVE FAITH IN YOURSELF.

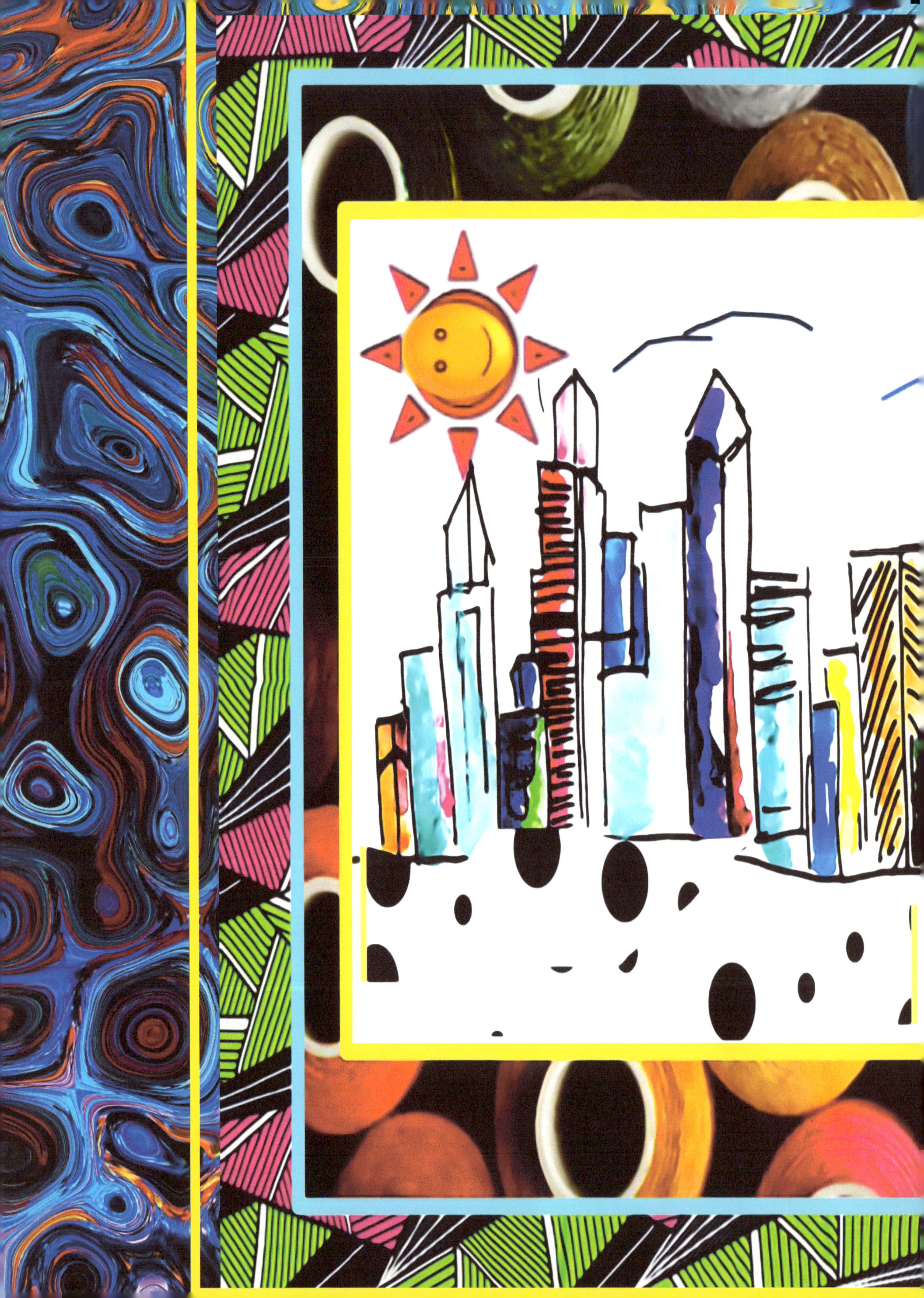

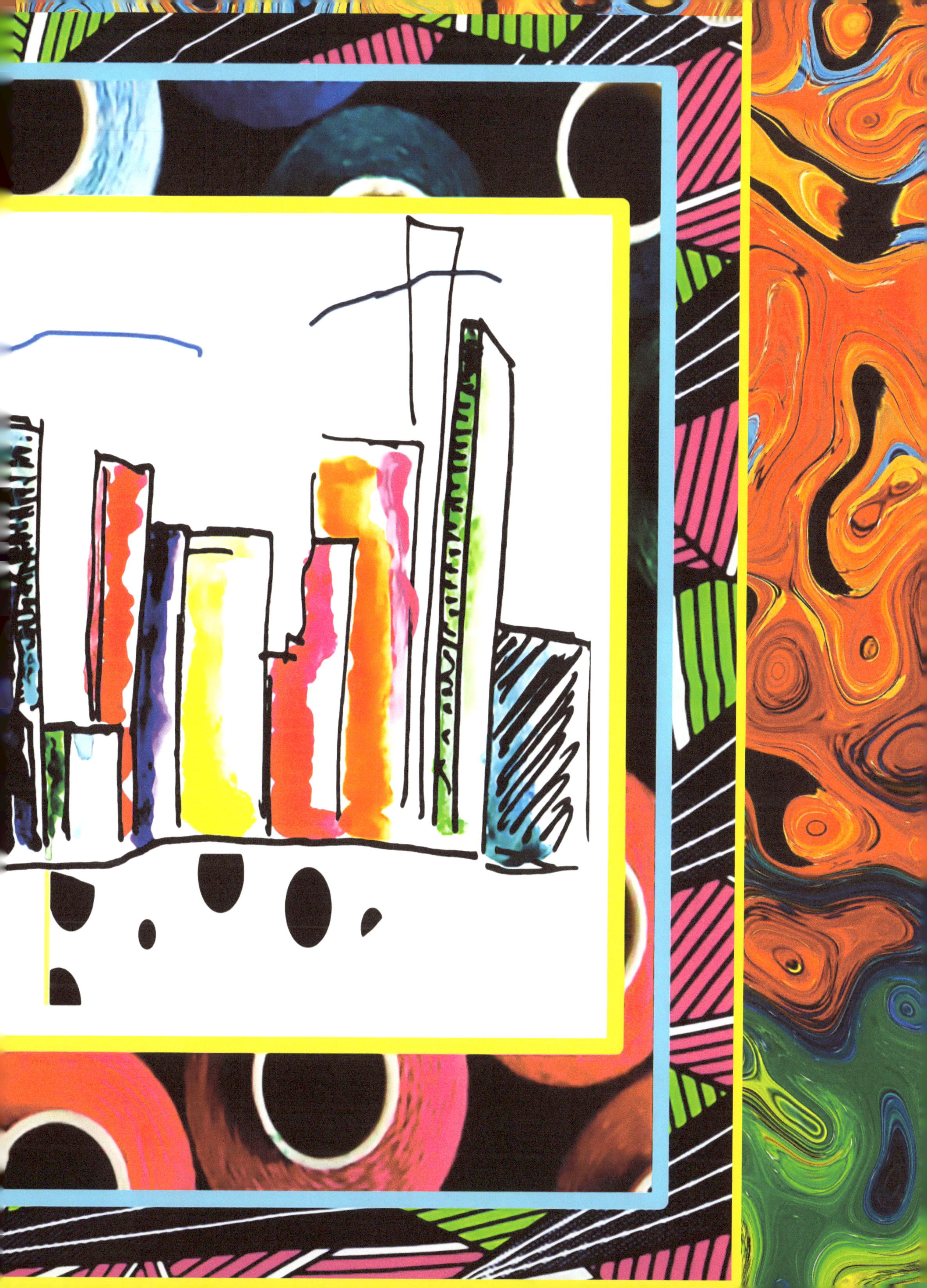

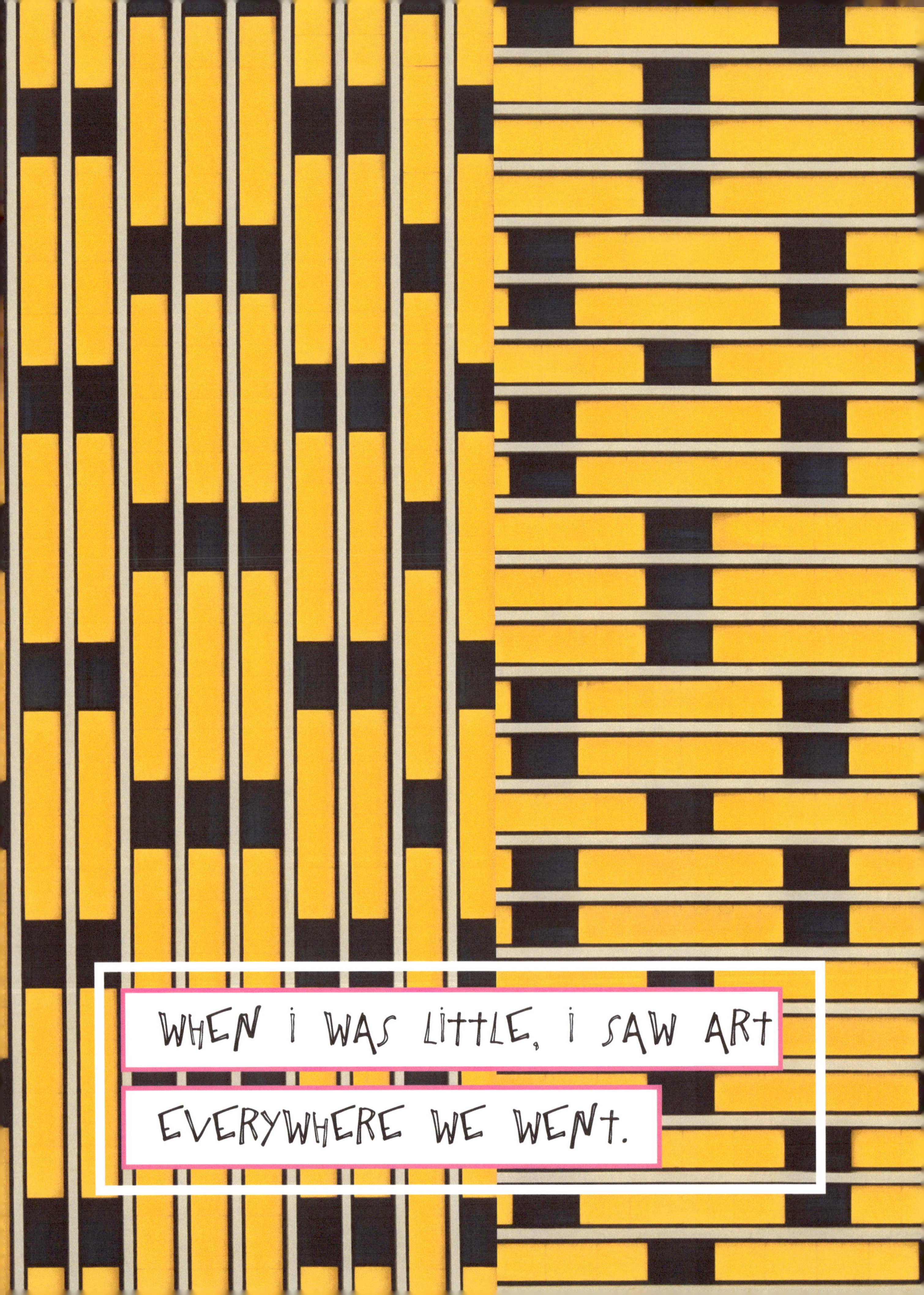
WHEN i WAS LiTTLE, i SAW ART
EVERYWHERE WE WENT.

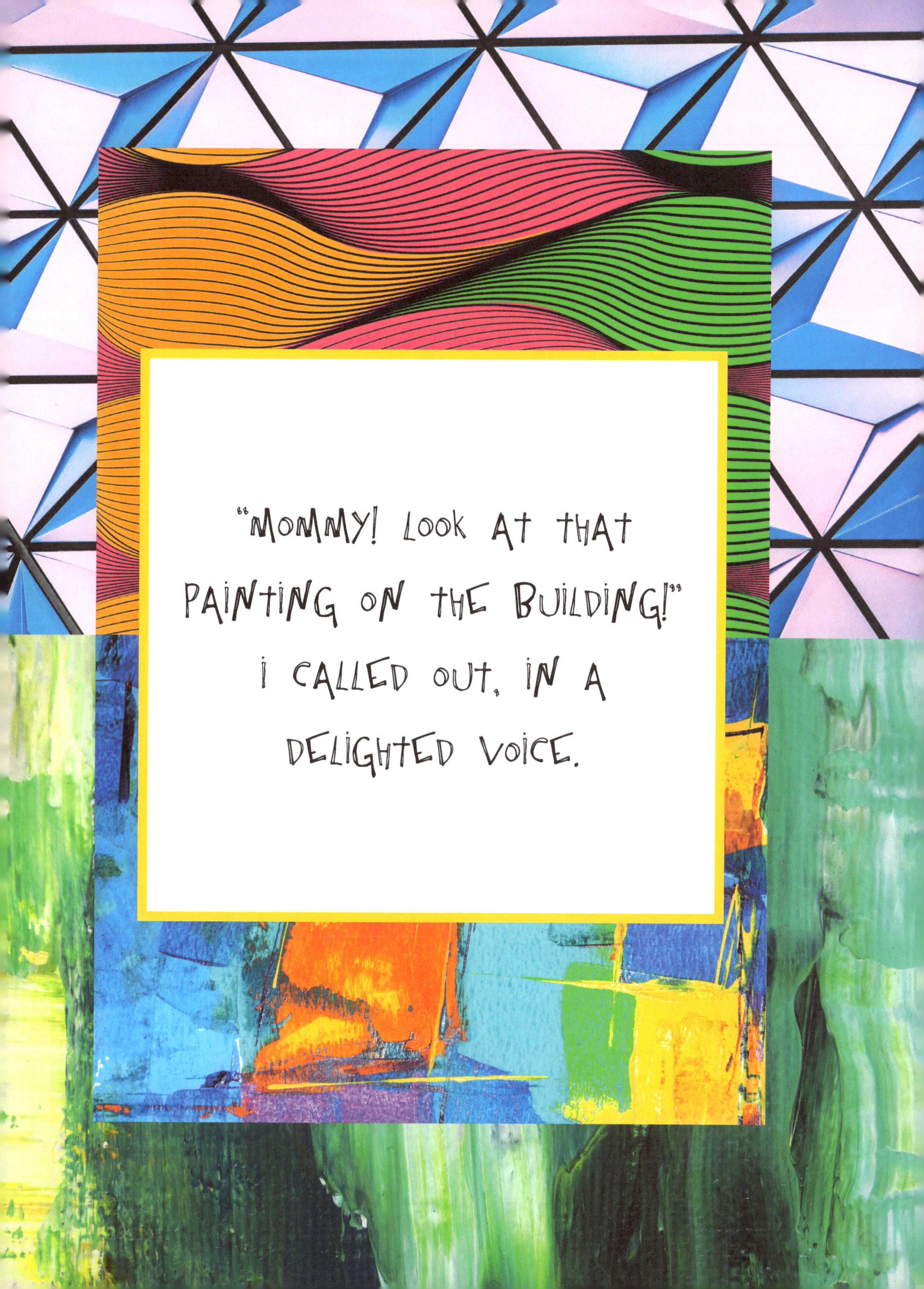
"MOMMY! LOOK AT THAT PAINTING ON THE BUILDING!" I CALLED OUT, IN A DELIGHTED VOICE.

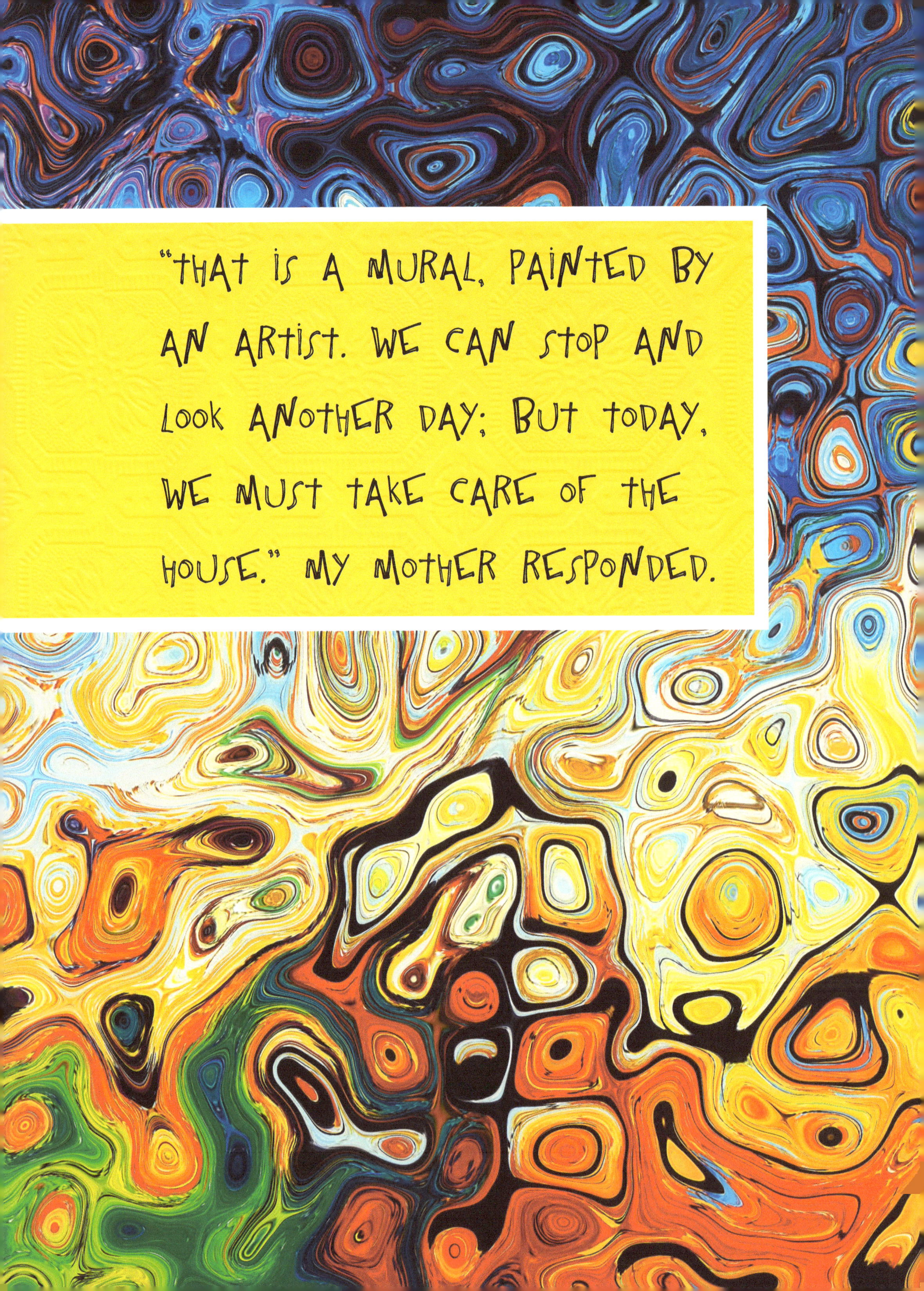

"THAT IS A MURAL, PAINTED BY AN ARTIST. WE CAN STOP AND LOOK ANOTHER DAY; BUT TODAY, WE MUST TAKE CARE OF THE HOUSE." MY MOTHER RESPONDED.

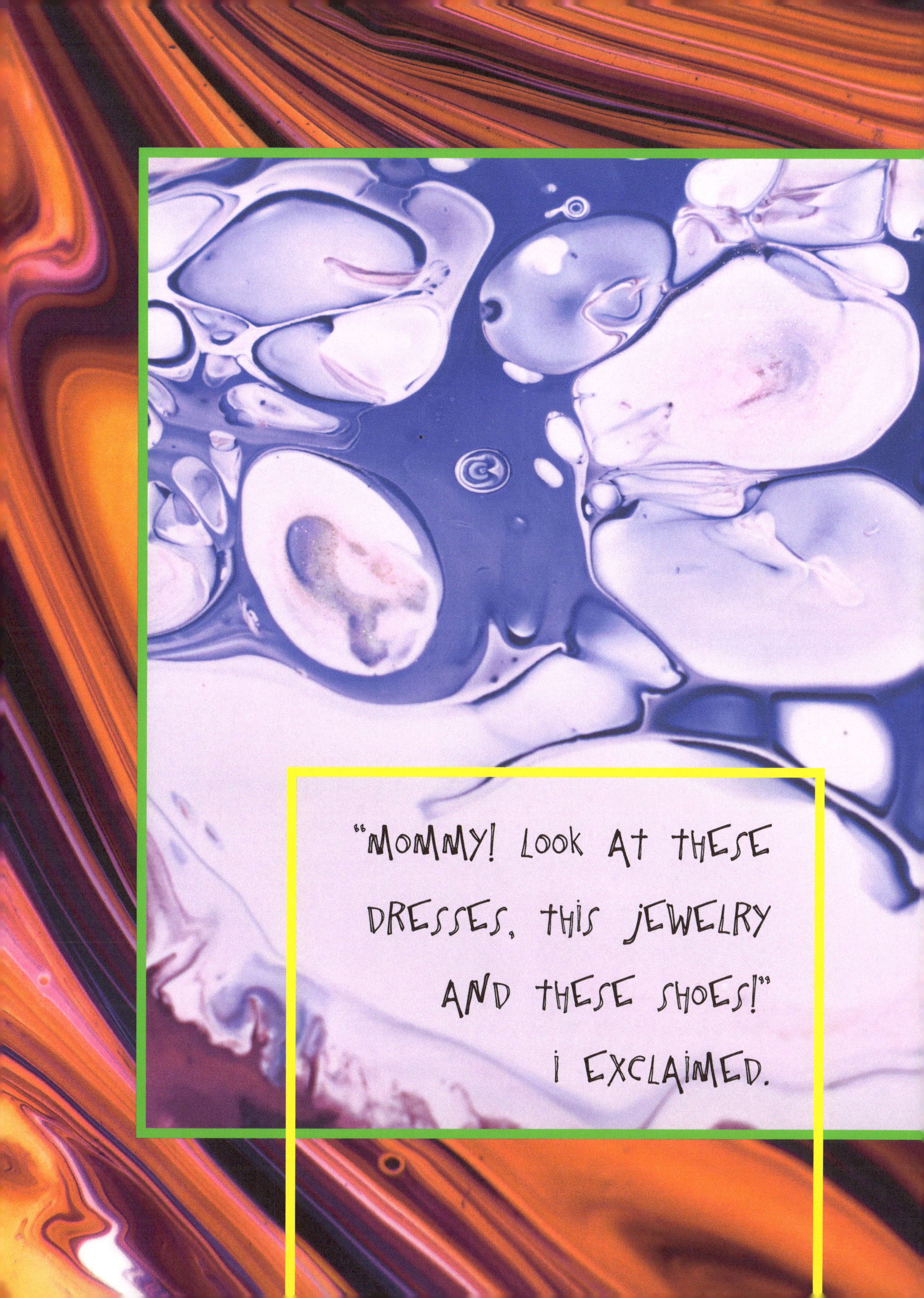
"MOMMY! LOOK AT THESE
DRESSES, THIS JEWELRY
AND THESE SHOES!"
I EXCLAIMED.

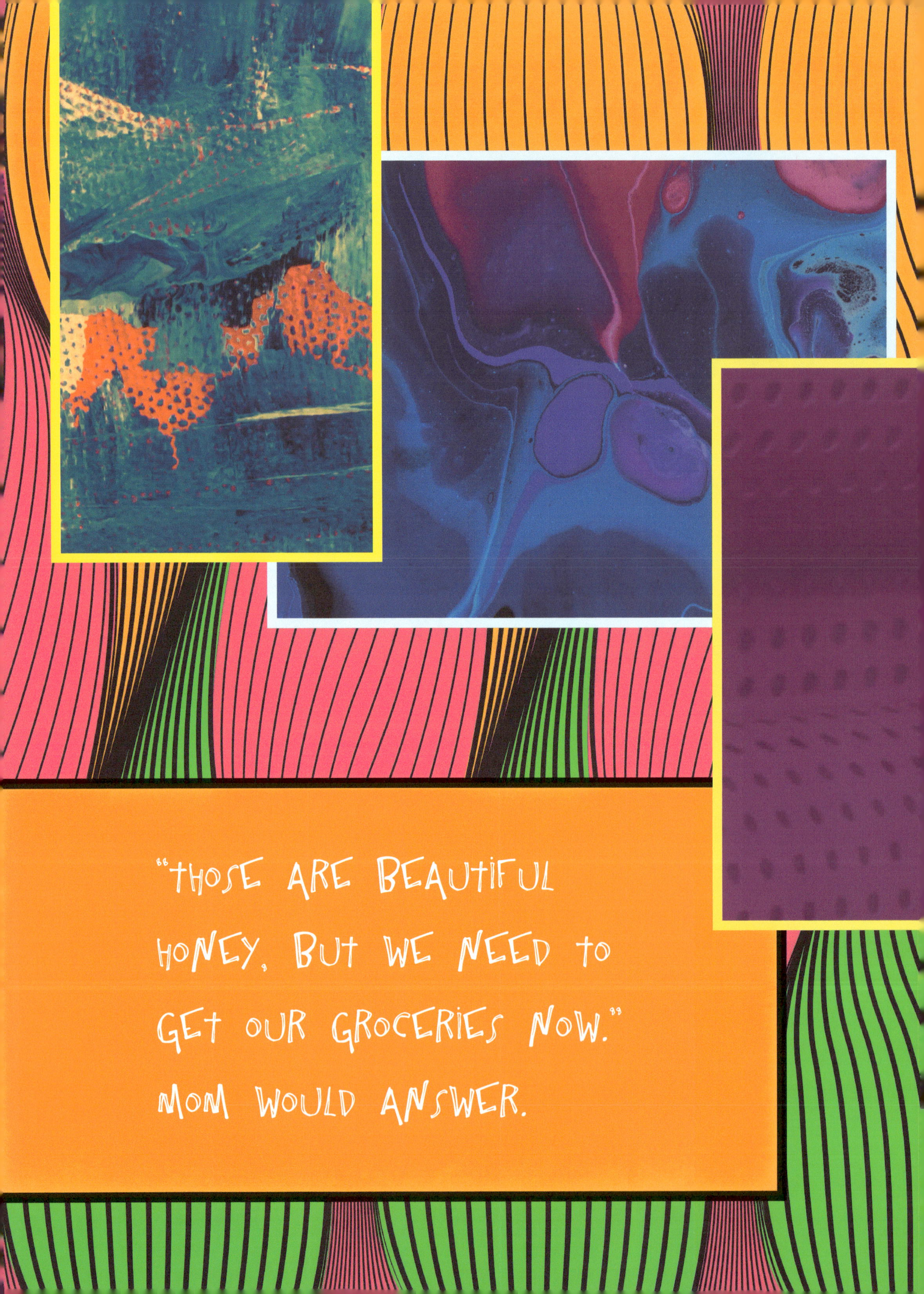
"Those are beautiful honey, but we need to get our groceries now." Mom would answer.

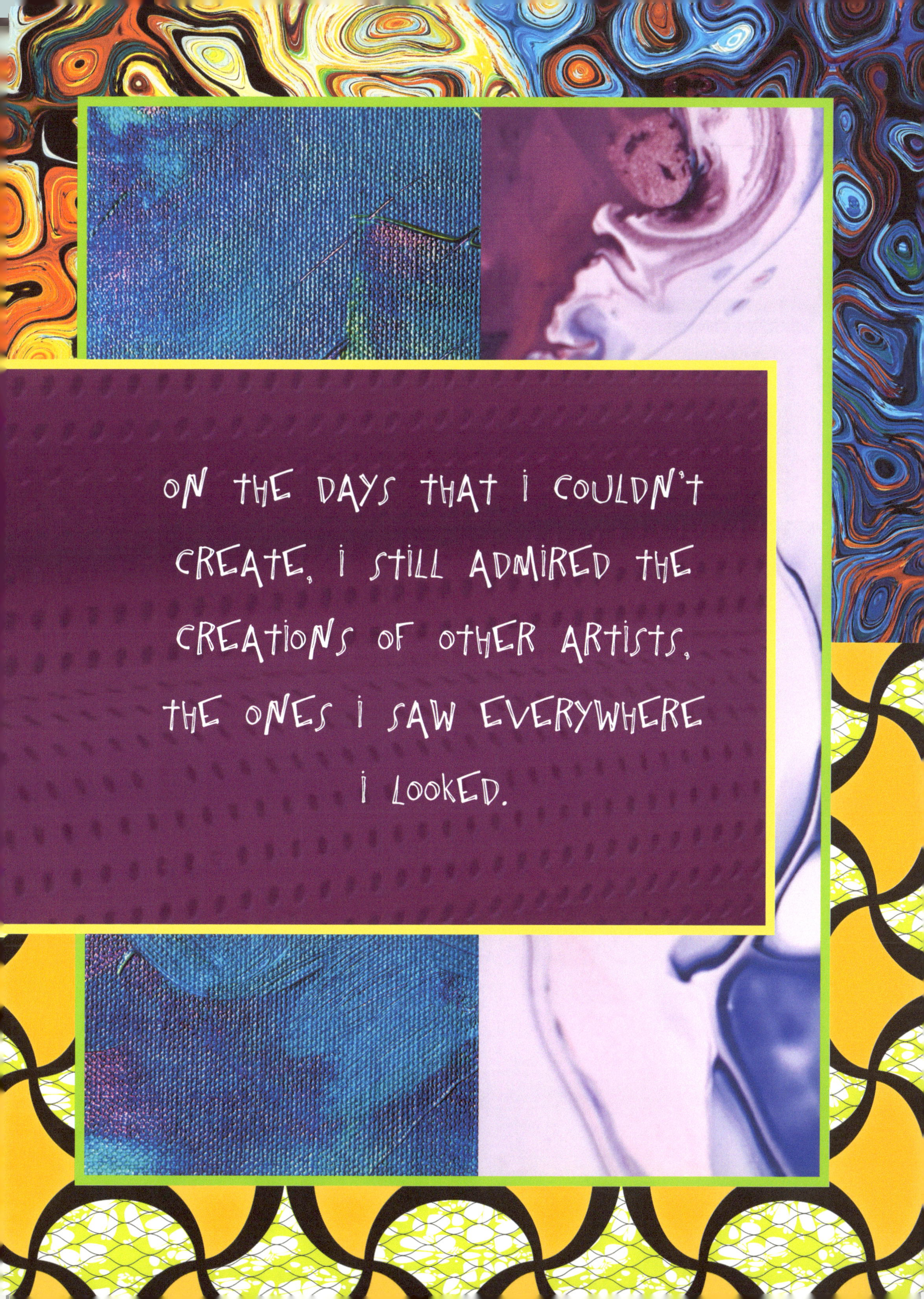

ON THE DAYS THAT I COULDN'T CREATE, I STILL ADMIRED THE CREATIONS OF OTHER ARTISTS, THE ONES I SAW EVERYWHERE I LOOKED.

HAVE YOU EVER SEEN A MURAL? WHAT WOULD YOU PAINT ON THE SIDE OF A BIG BUILDING?

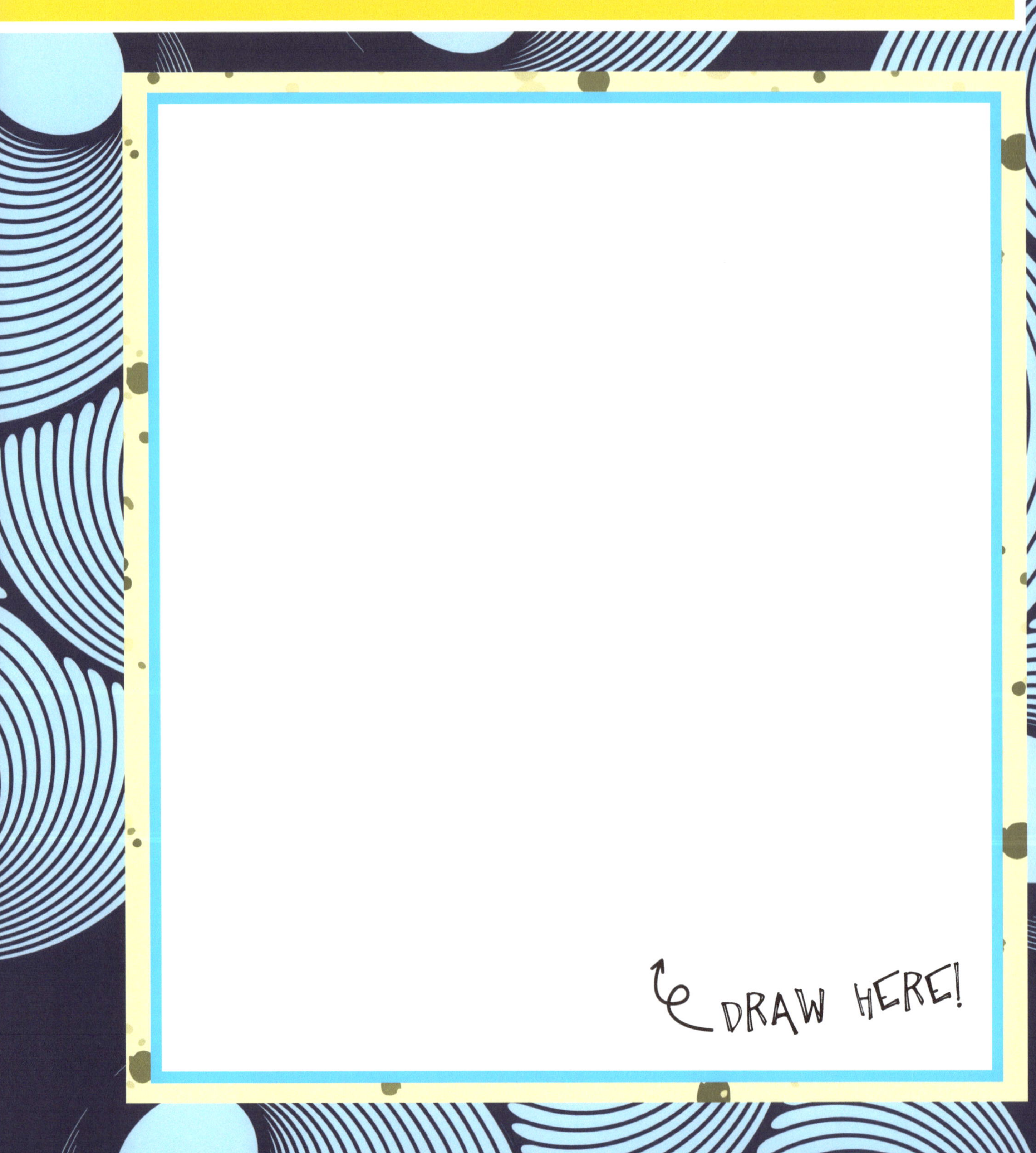

HAVE YOU EVER SEEN CLOTHING THAT LOOKED LIKE ART TO YOU? DESIGN THE MOST ARTISTIC OUTFIT YOU CAN IMAGINE!

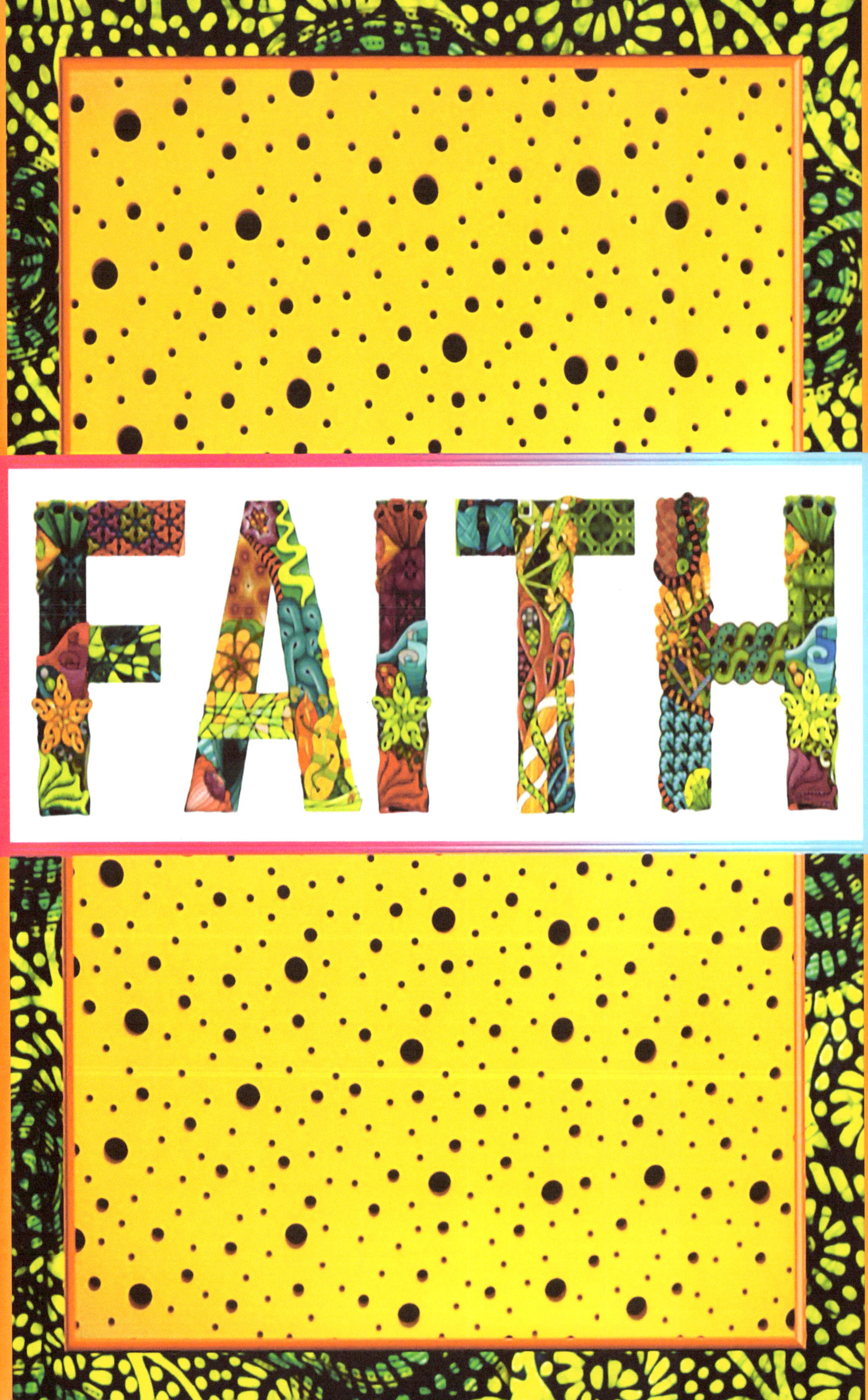

FAITH

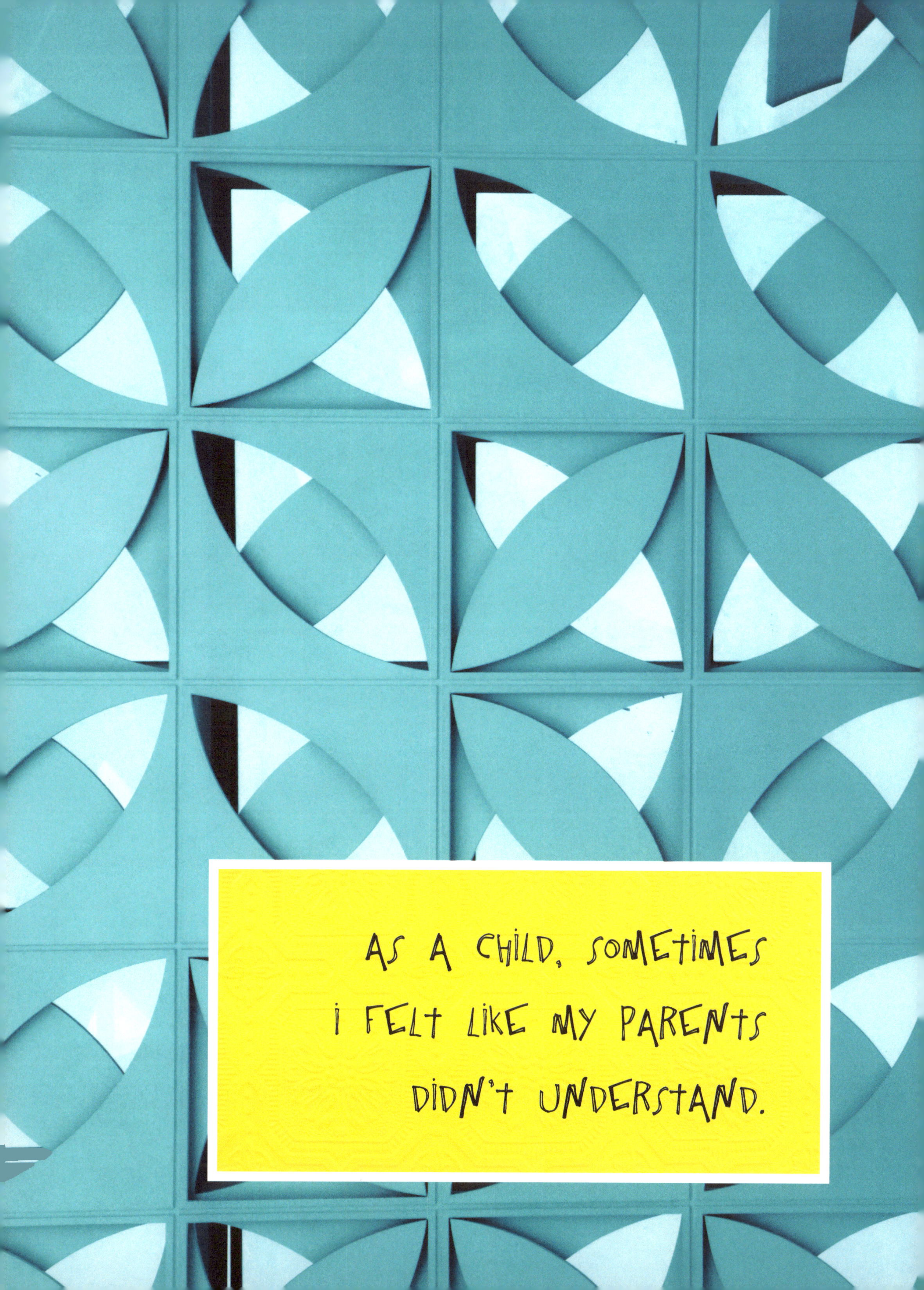

AS A CHILD, SOMETIMES
I FELT LIKE MY PARENTS
DIDN'T UNDERSTAND.

"MAJARA! NO! WE DON'T HAVE TIME FOR THIS!" THEY WOULD SAY.

"MOM, WHEN WILL I HAVE MORE TIME FOR MY ART?" I ASKED

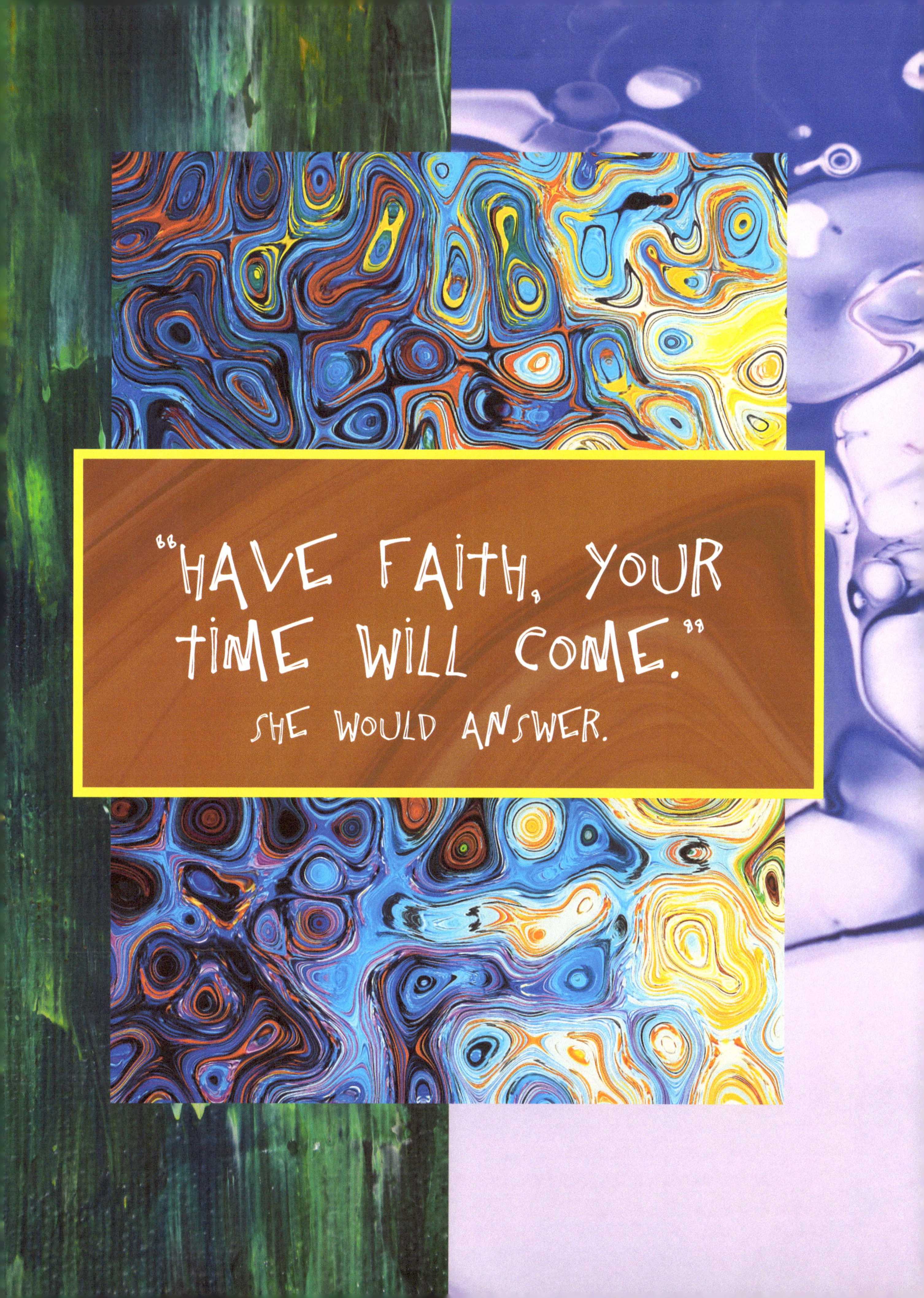

"HAVE FAITH, YOUR TIME WILL COME."
SHE WOULD ANSWER.

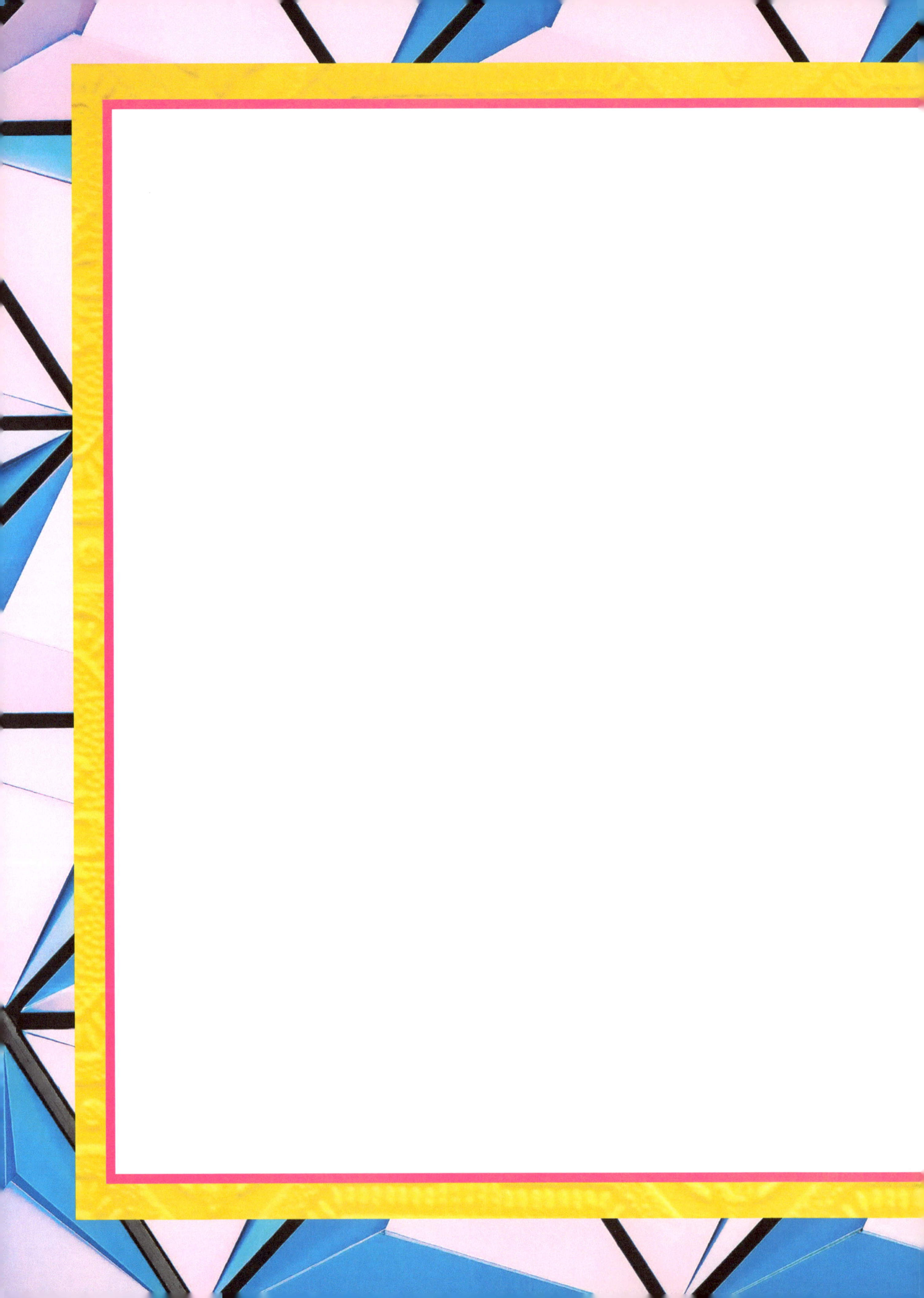

CREATE HERE!

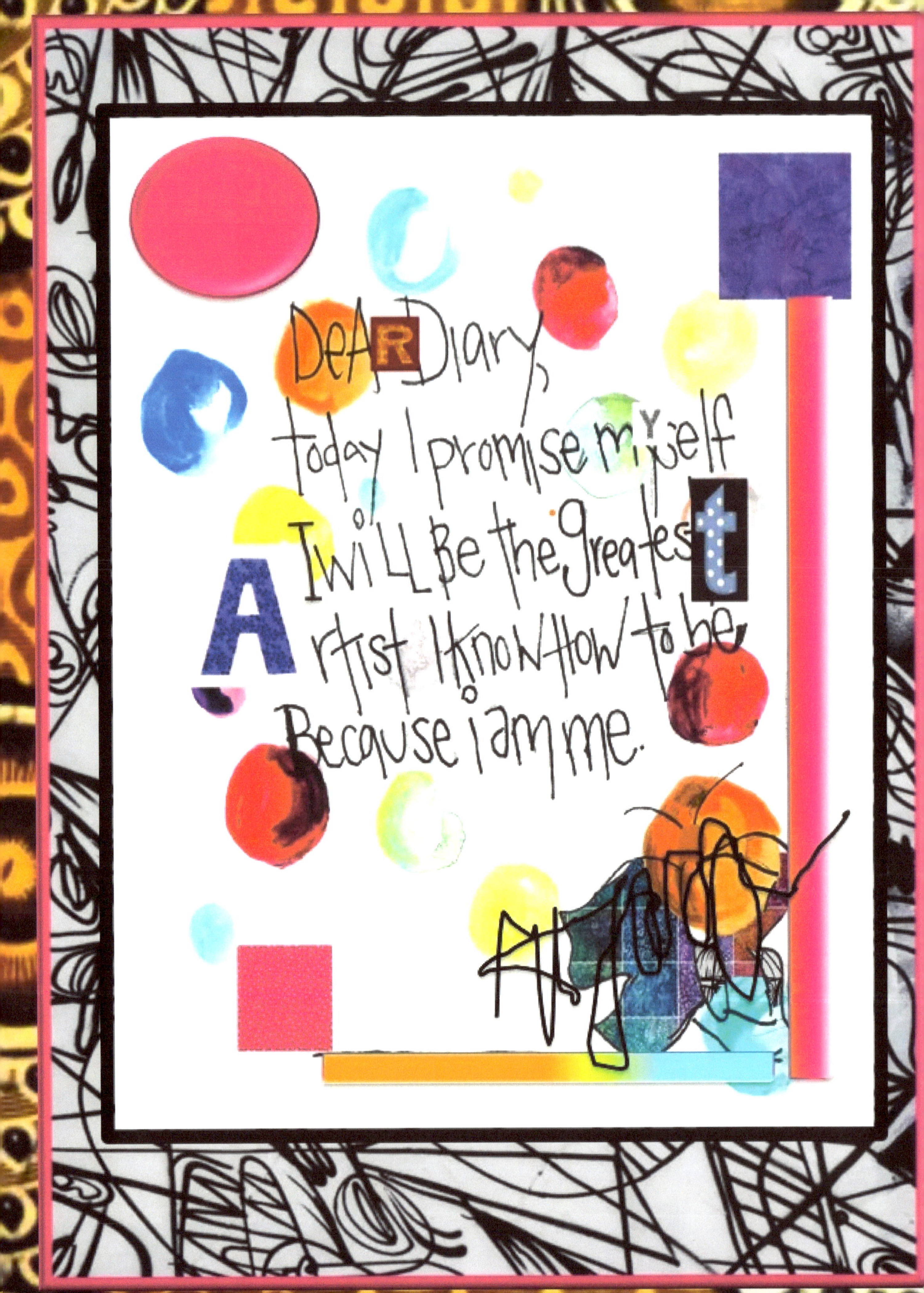
DeAR Diary,
today I promise myself
I will Be the greatest
Artist I know How to be
Because i am me.

When times are hard,
and I am stressed, I
write in my journal.

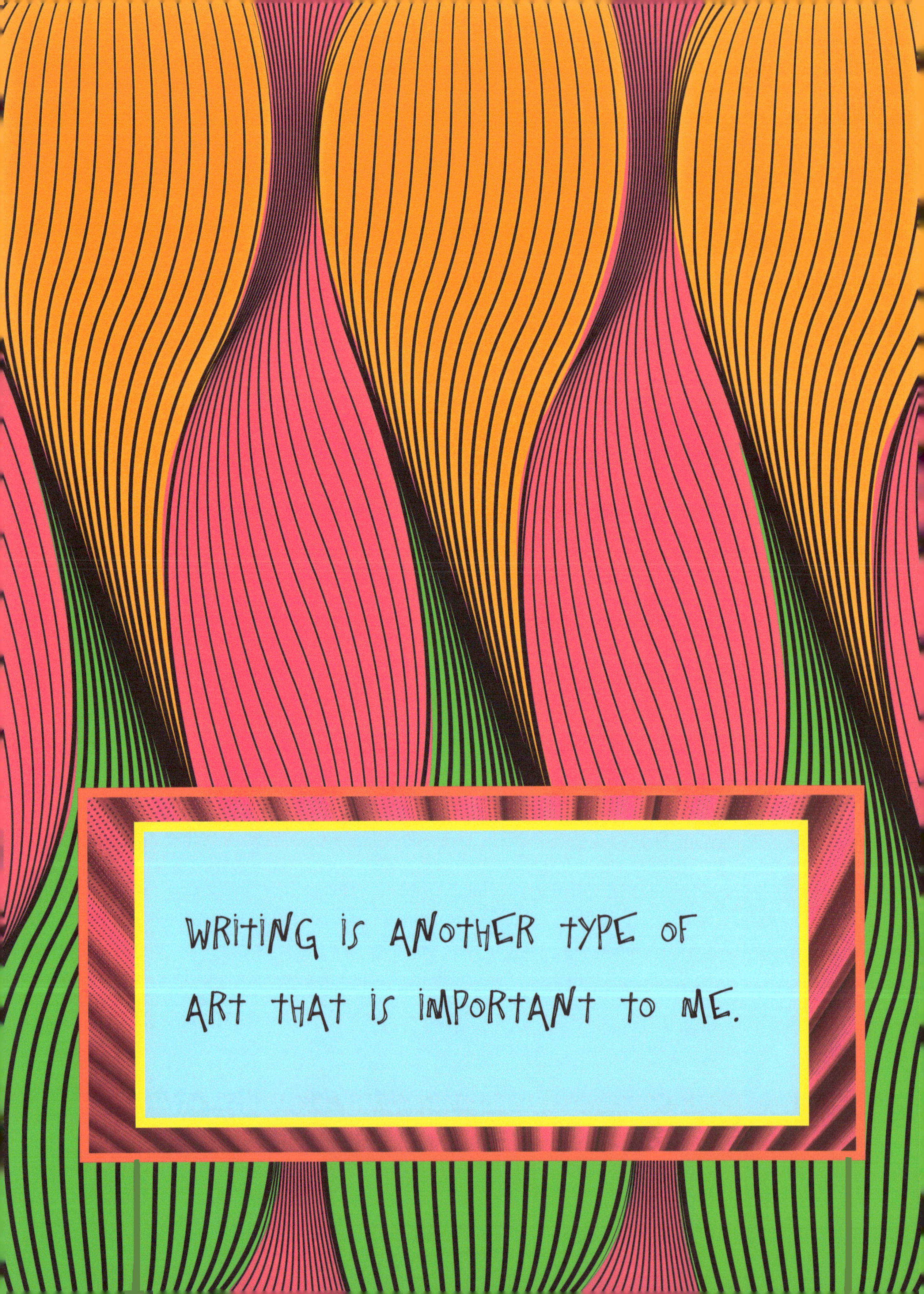
WRITING IS ANOTHER TYPE OF
ART THAT IS IMPORTANT TO ME.

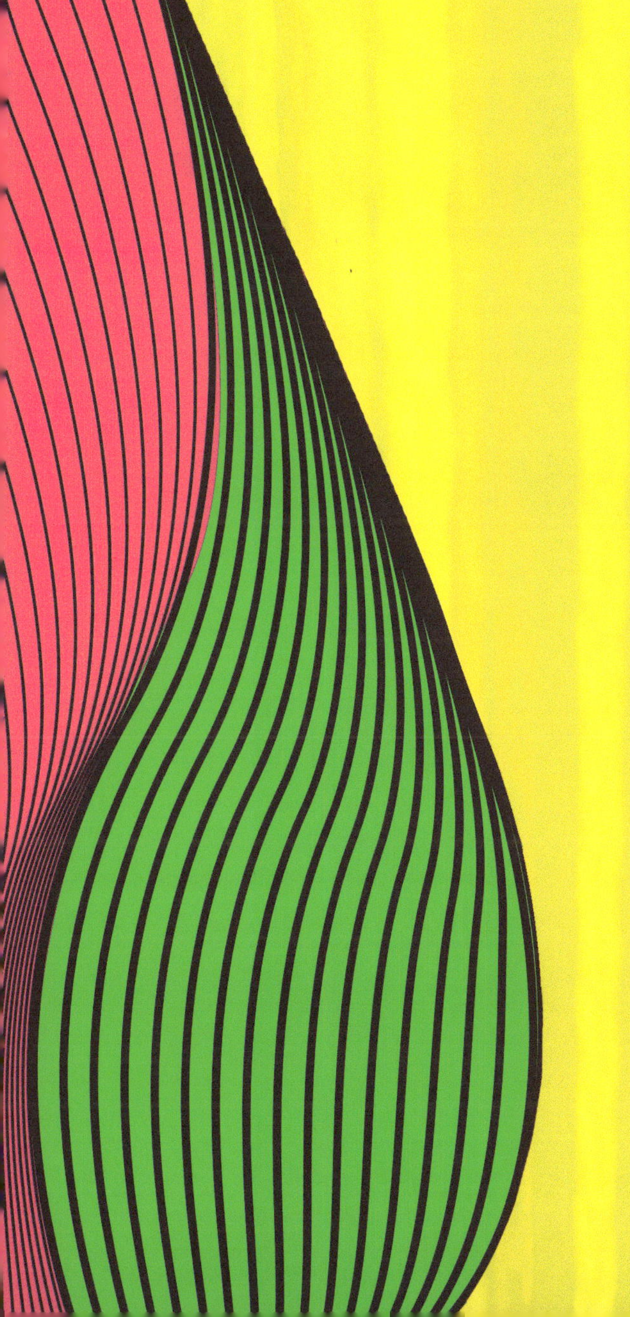

i WRITE EVERYTHING ON PAPER;
i WRITE ABOUT MY FEELINGS,
MY FEARS, AND MY DREAMS.

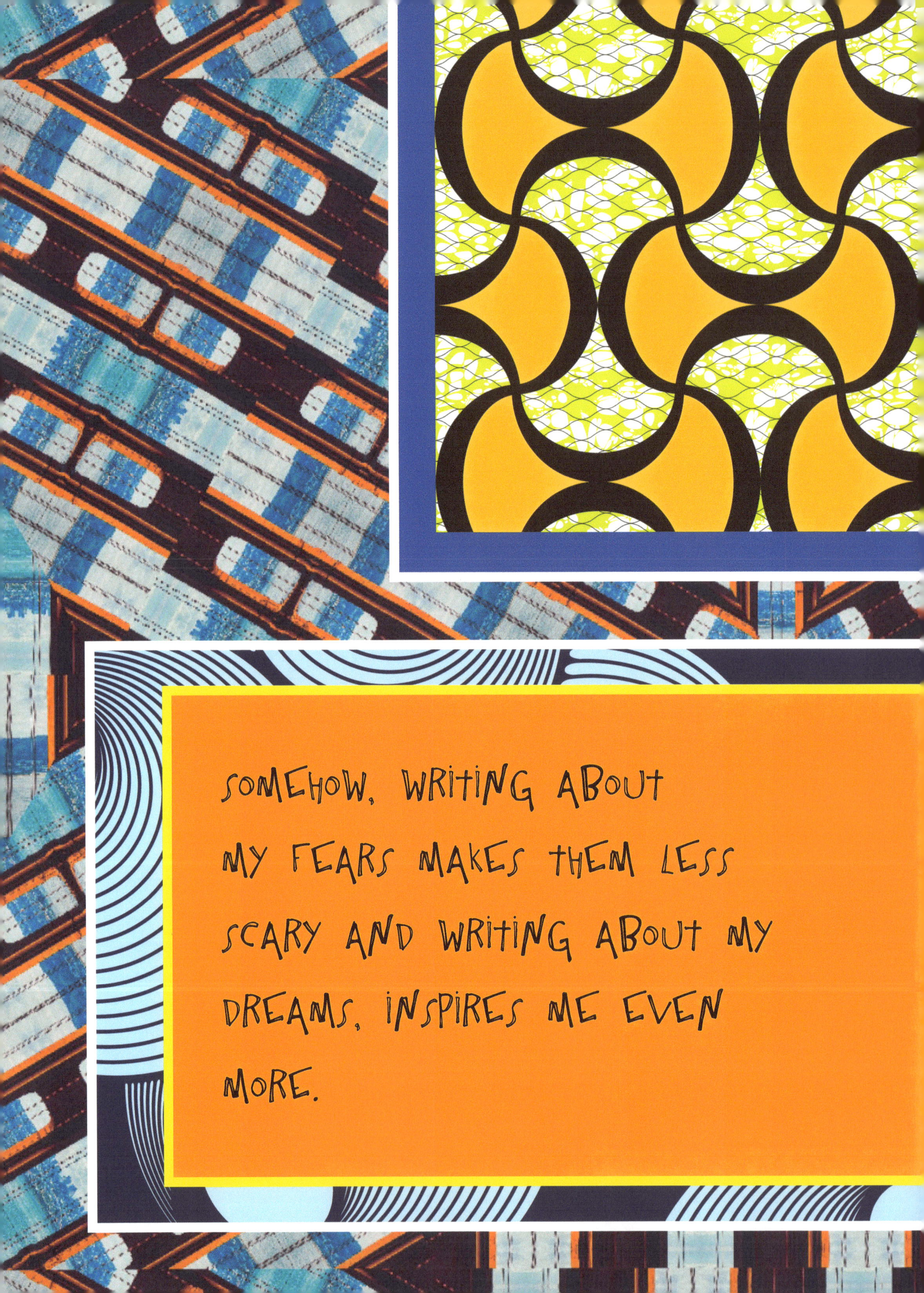

SOMEHOW, WRITING ABOUT MY FEARS MAKES THEM LESS SCARY AND WRITING ABOUT MY DREAMS, INSPIRES ME EVEN MORE.

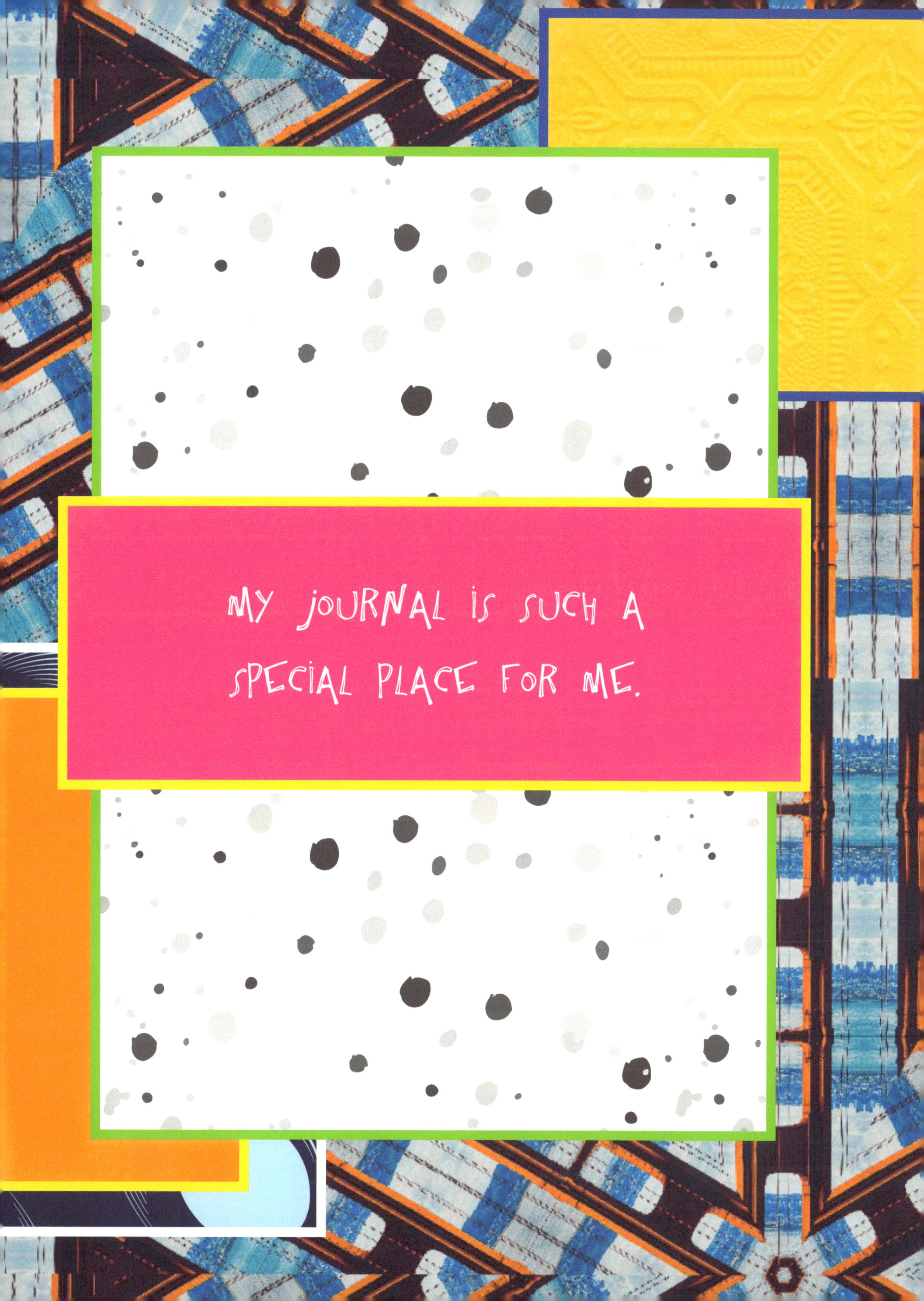

MY JOURNAL IS SUCH A
SPECIAL PLACE FOR ME.

WRITE DOWN YOUR DREAMS, YOUR
FEELINGS, YOUR STORY, AND YOUR
FEARS. OR, WRITE DOWN WHATEVER
YOU WANT!

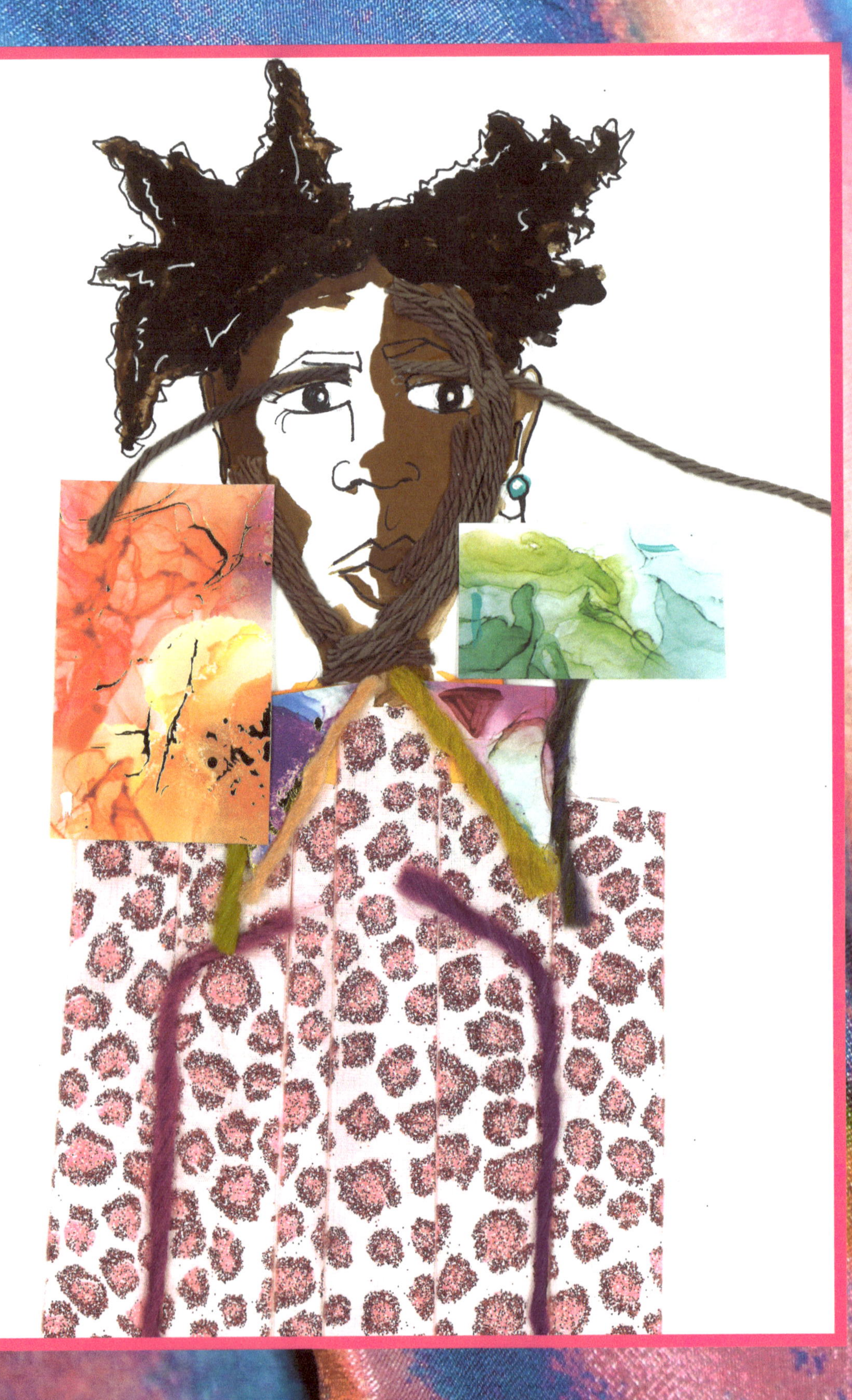

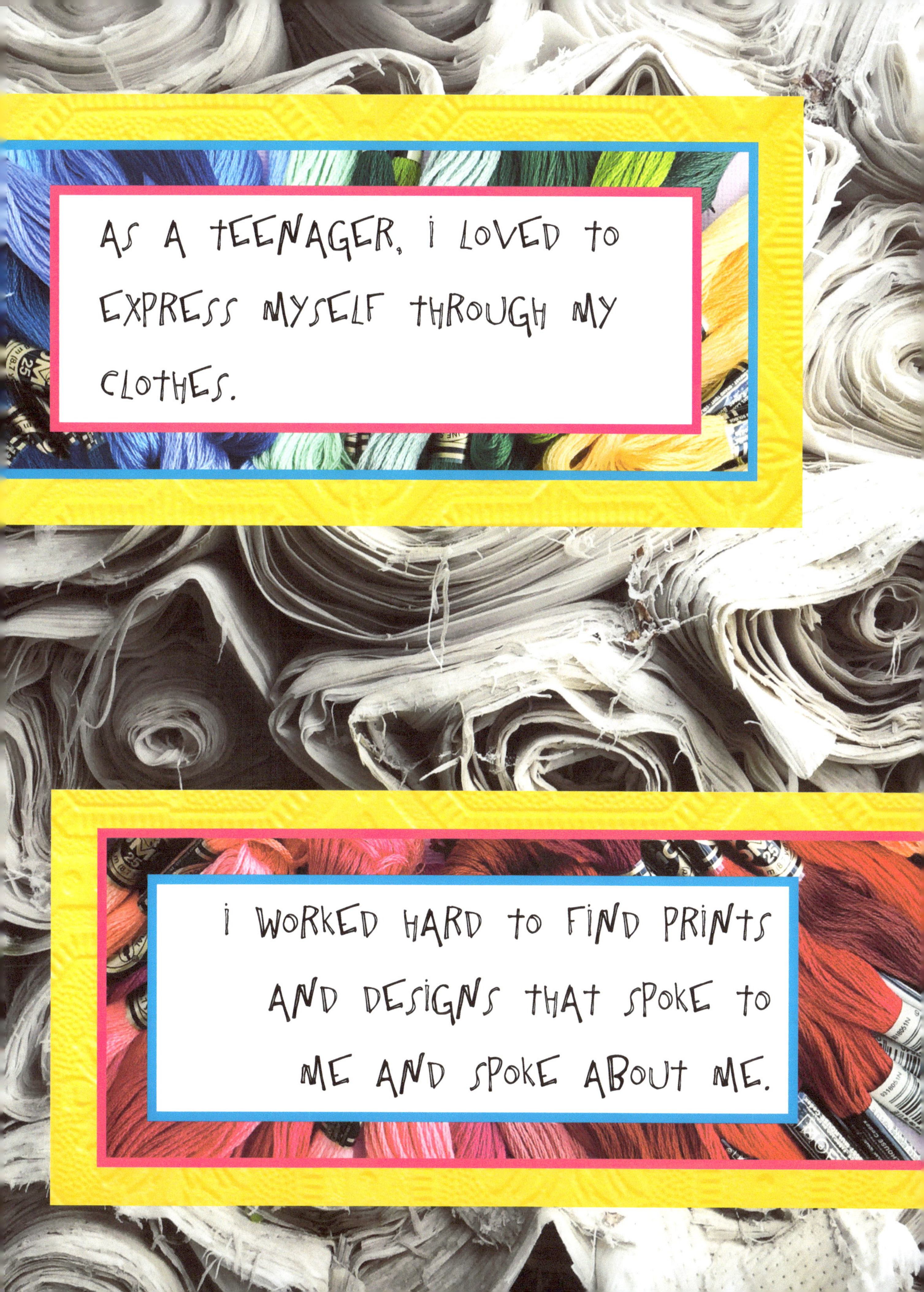
AS A TEENAGER, I LOVED TO EXPRESS MYSELF THROUGH MY CLOTHES.

I WORKED HARD TO FIND PRINTS AND DESIGNS THAT SPOKE TO ME AND SPOKE ABOUT ME.

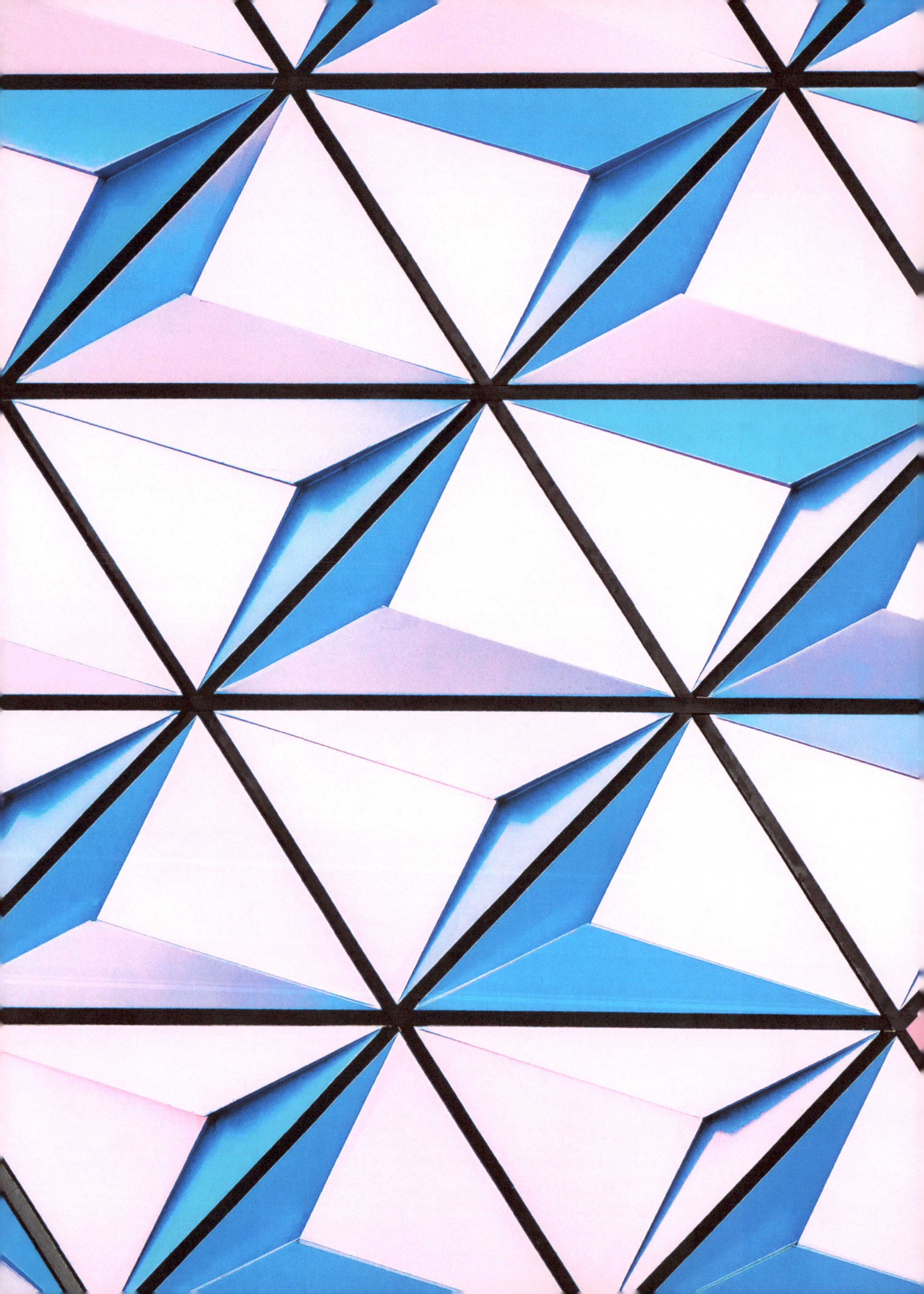

WHAT I WORE WAS A
STATEMENT OF MY
LOVE FOR ART!

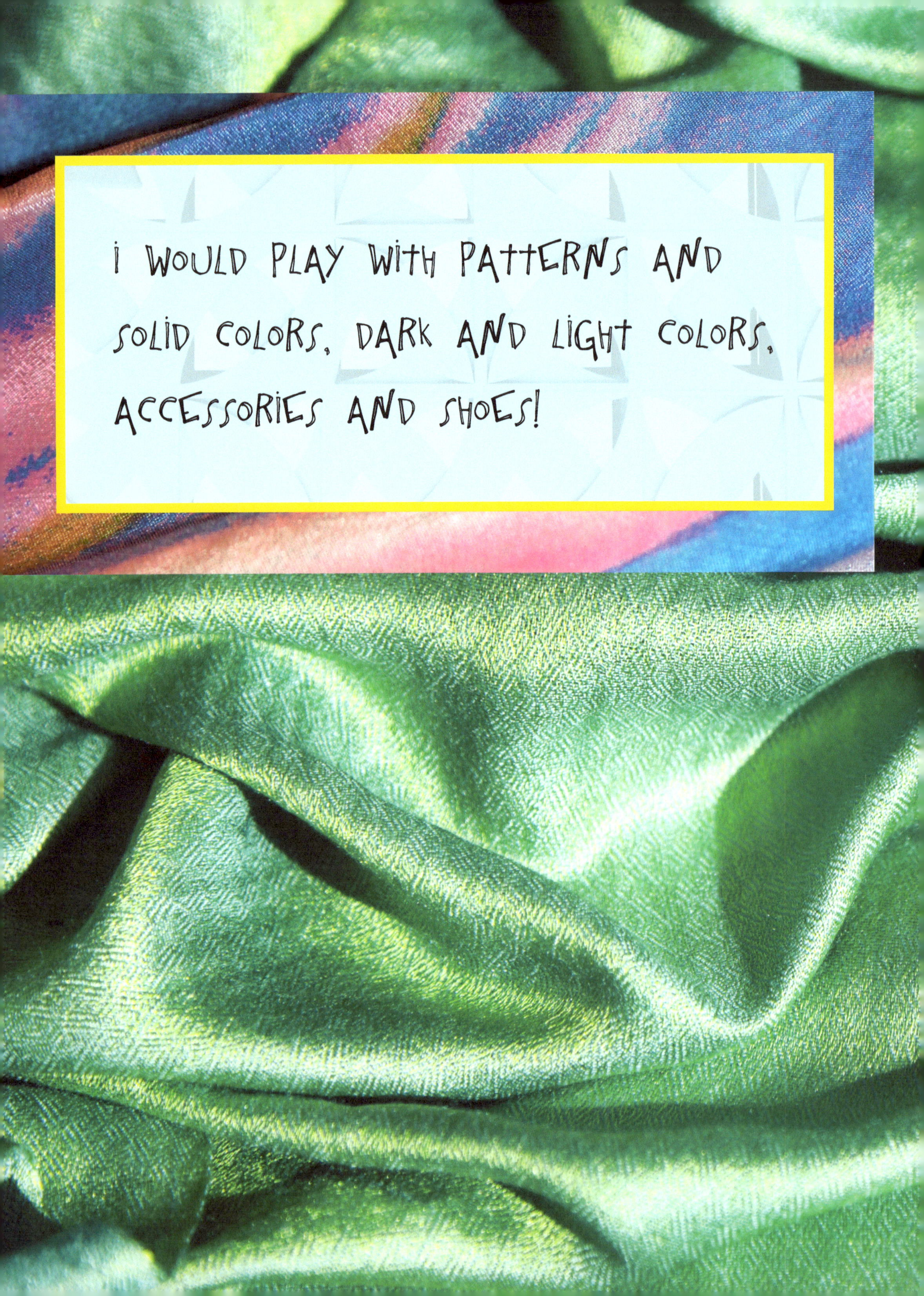

i WOULD PLAY WITH PATTERNS AND
SOLID COLORS, DARK AND LIGHT COLORS,
ACCESSORIES AND SHOES!

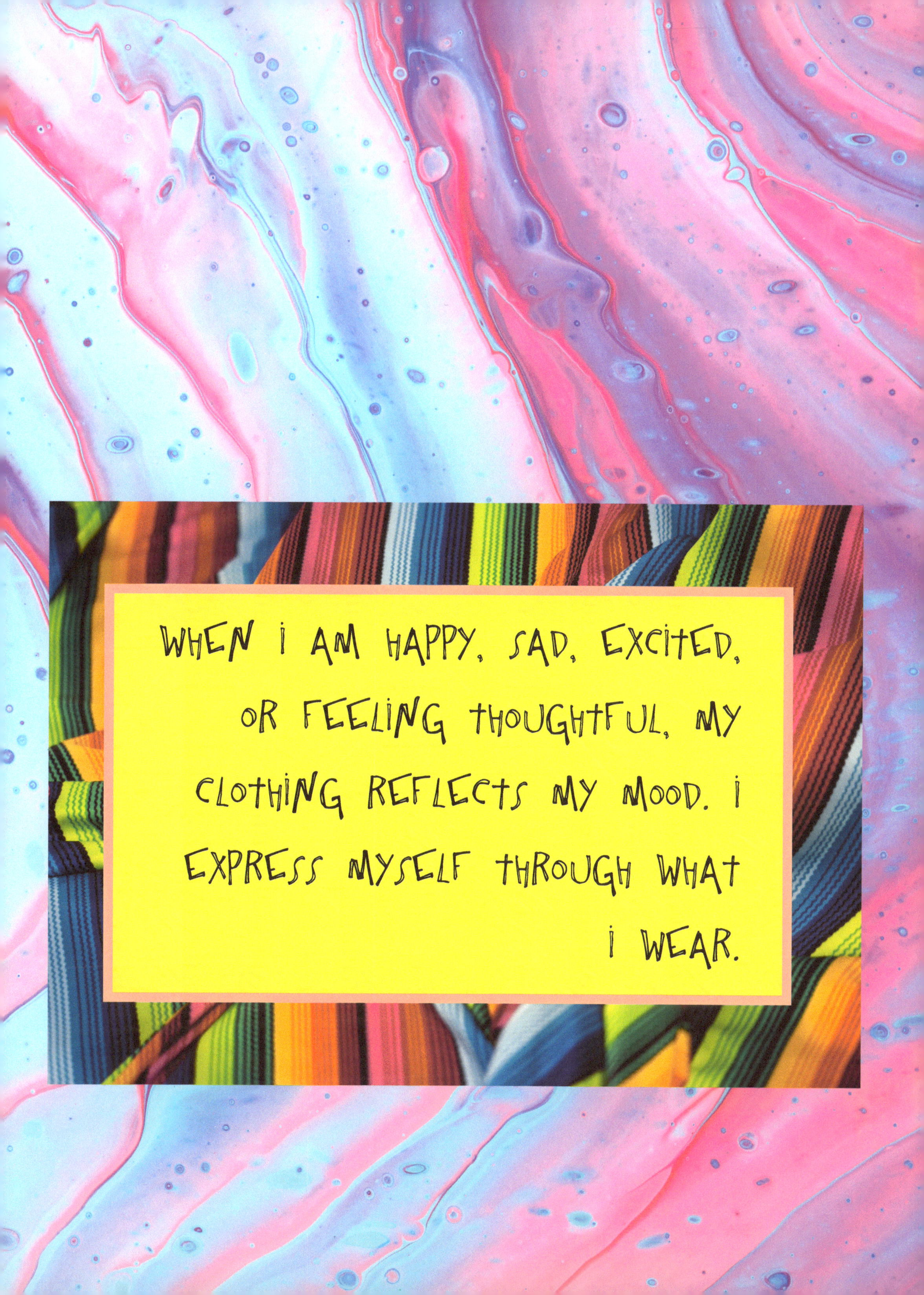

WHEN i AM HAPPY, SAD, EXCITED,
OR FEELING thOUGHTFUL, MY
clOthiNG REFLECtS MY MOOD. i
EXPRESS MYSELF thROUGH WHAT
i WEAR.

WHAT DO YOU WEAR WHEN.....

DRAW HERE!

... YOU WANT to BE NOTICED?

DRAW HERE!

..YOU ARE FEELING THOUGHTFUL?

DRAW HERE!

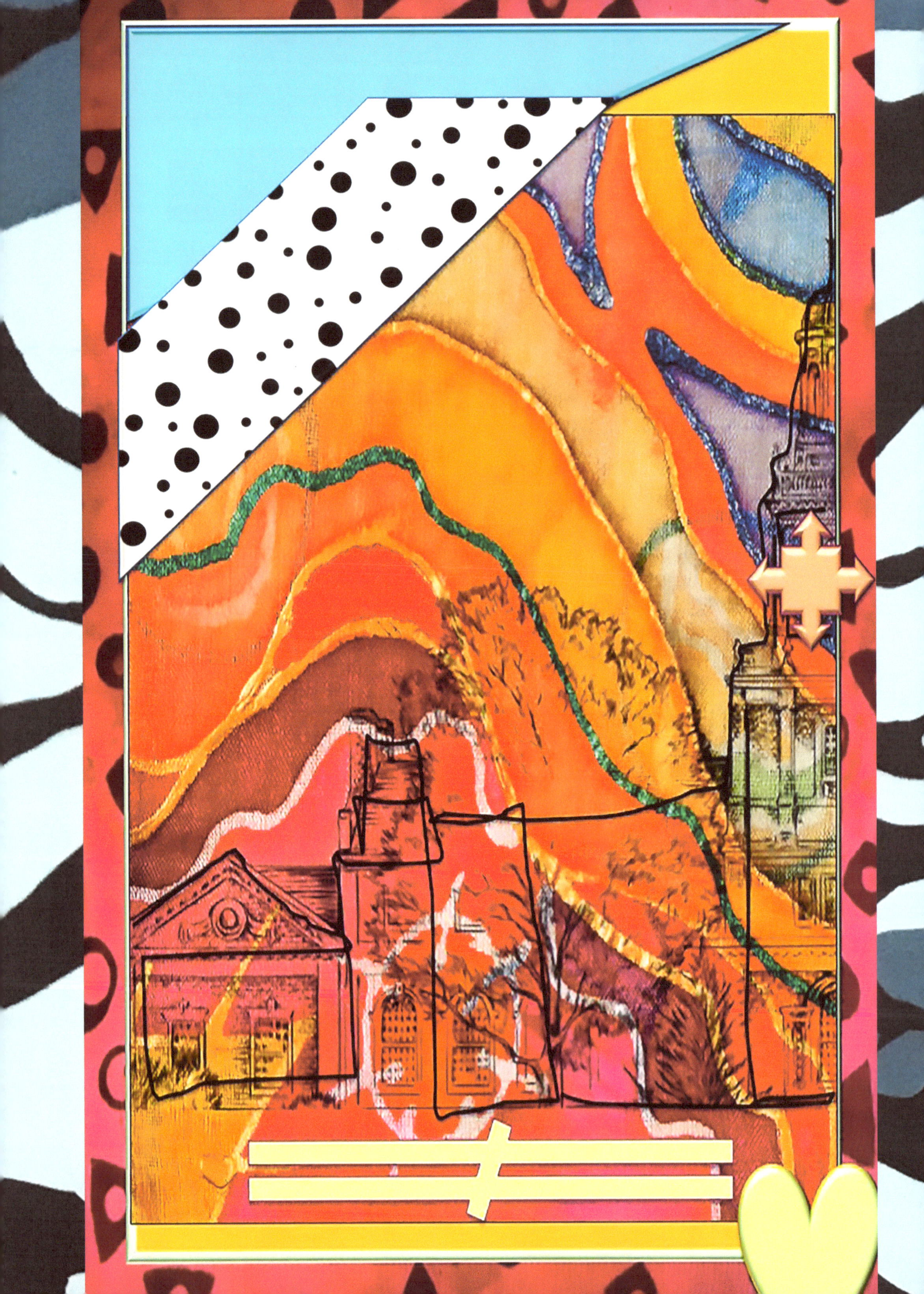

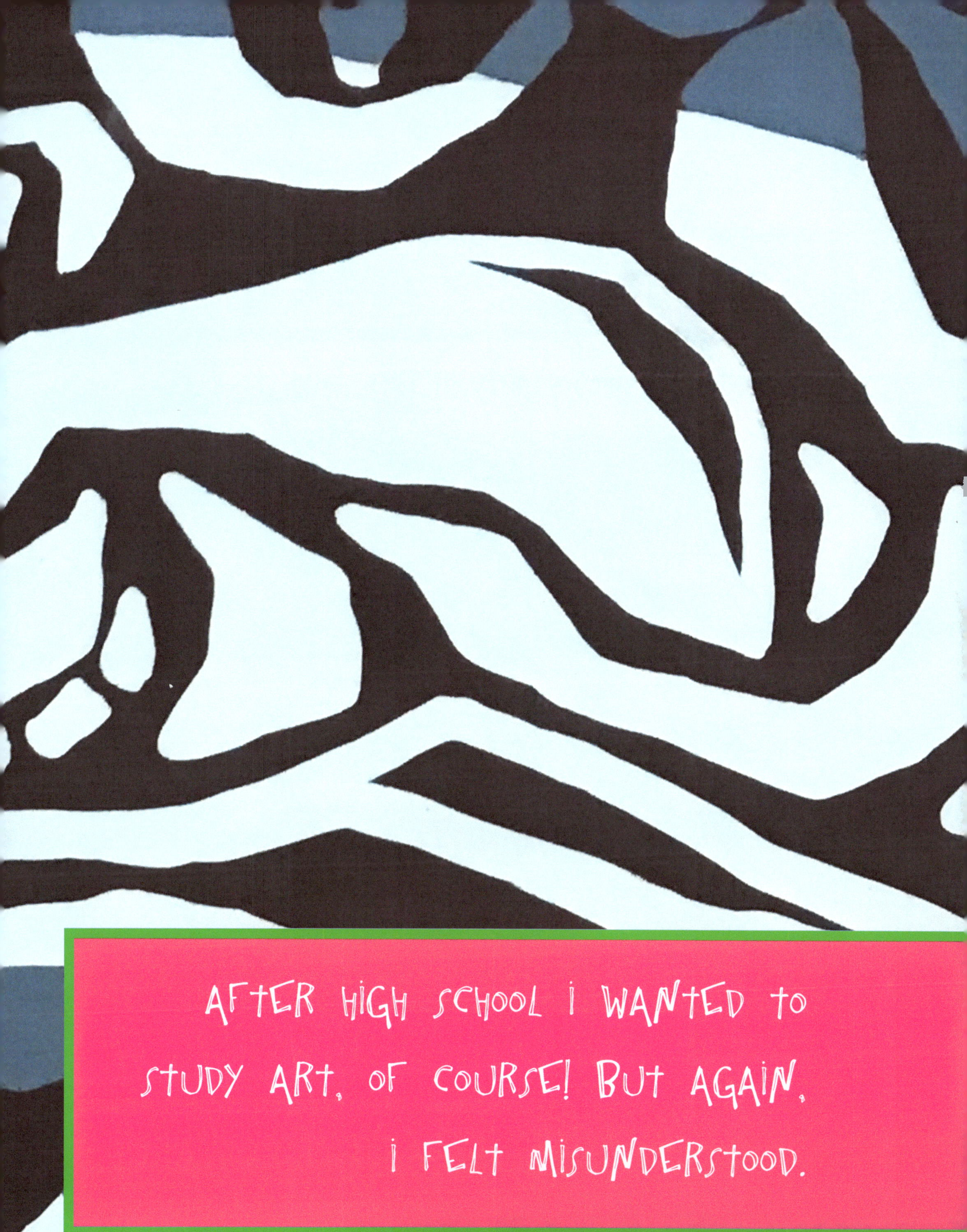

AFTER HIGH SCHOOL I WANTED TO STUDY ART, OF COURSE! BUT AGAIN, I FELT MISUNDERSTOOD.

"YOU NEED TO STUDY BUSINESS!

IT WILL HELP YOU TO GET A GOOD

JOB." MY PARENTS EXPLAINED.

"I WANT TO KEEP WORKING ON

MY ART!" I DECLARED.

"YOU CAN DO YOUR ART AFTER WORK; YOU CAN MAKE ART ON THE WEEKENDS. YOU NEED A SMART DEGREE AND A GOOD JOB."
MY PARENTS DECIDED.

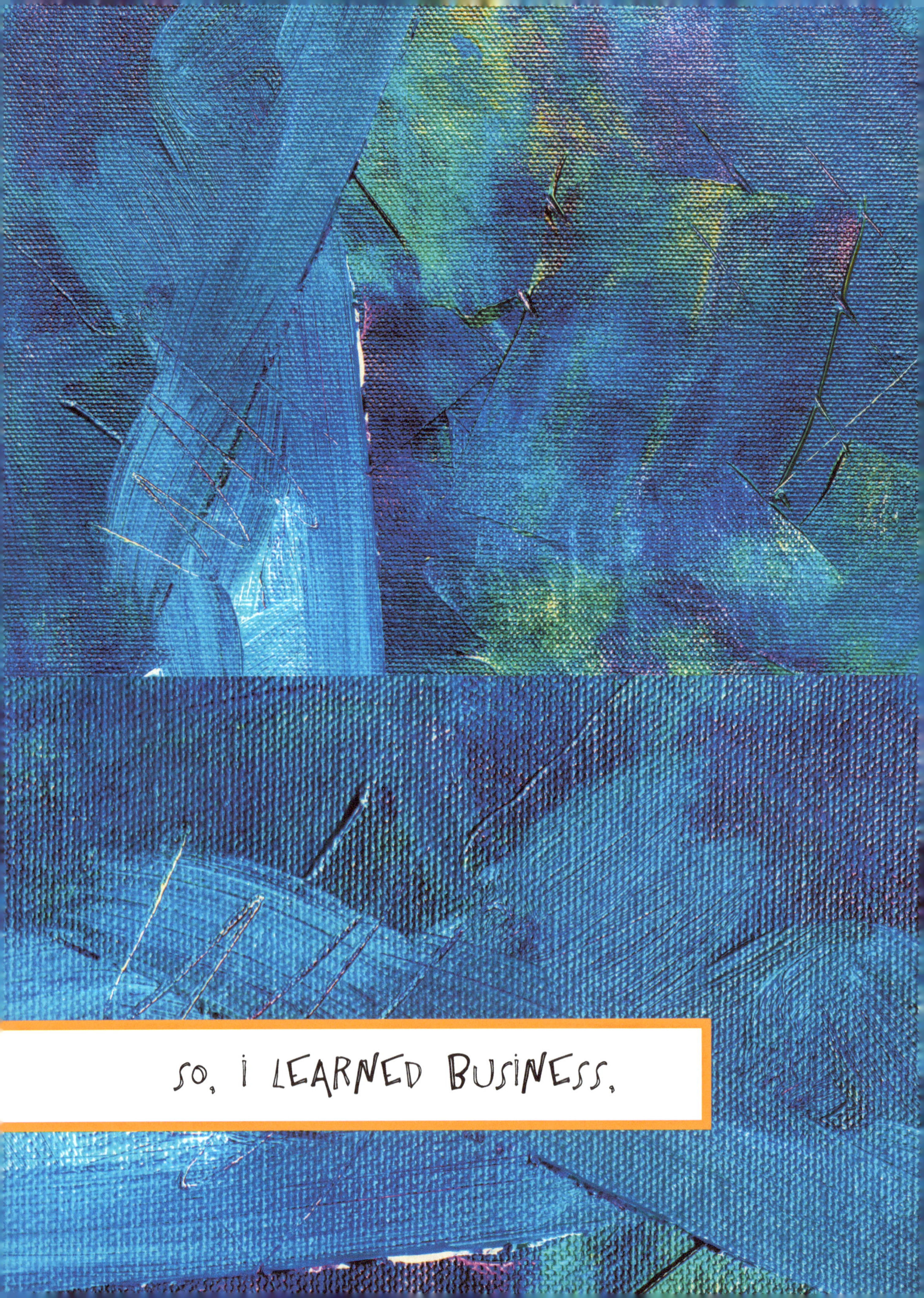

SO, i LEARNED BUSINESS.

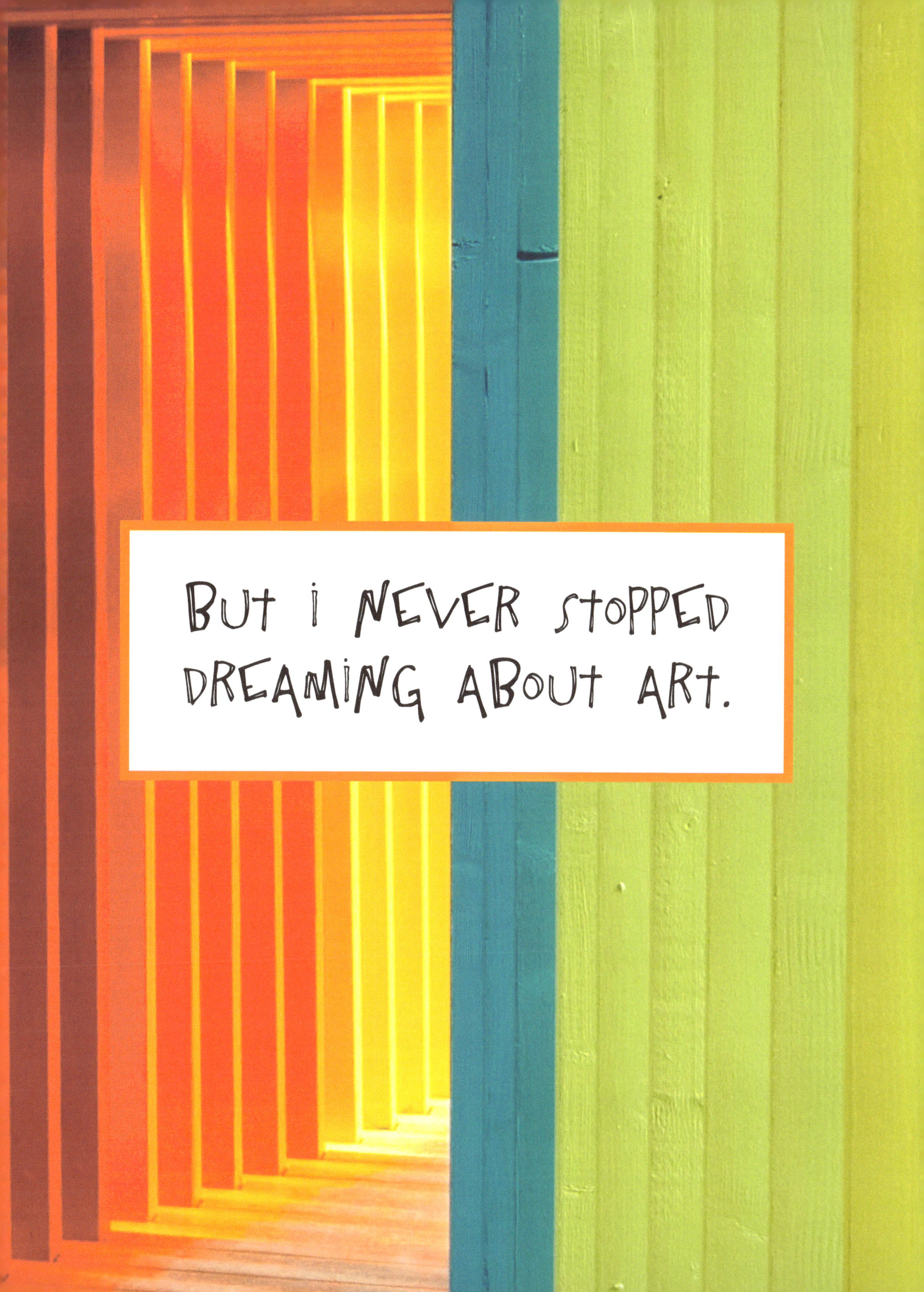
BUT I NEVER STOPPED DREAMING ABOUT ART.

WRITE OR DRAW YOUR DREAMS HERE

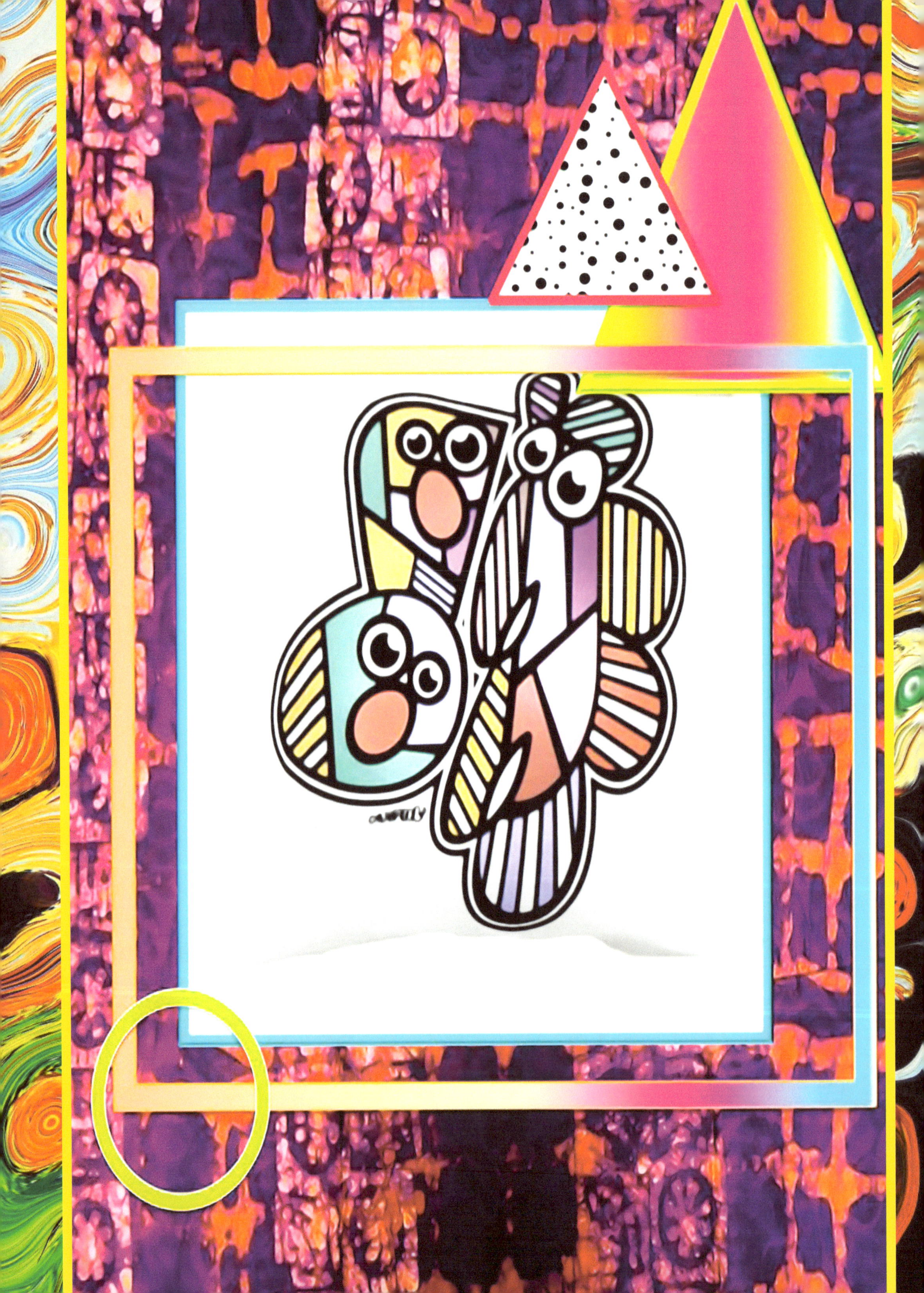

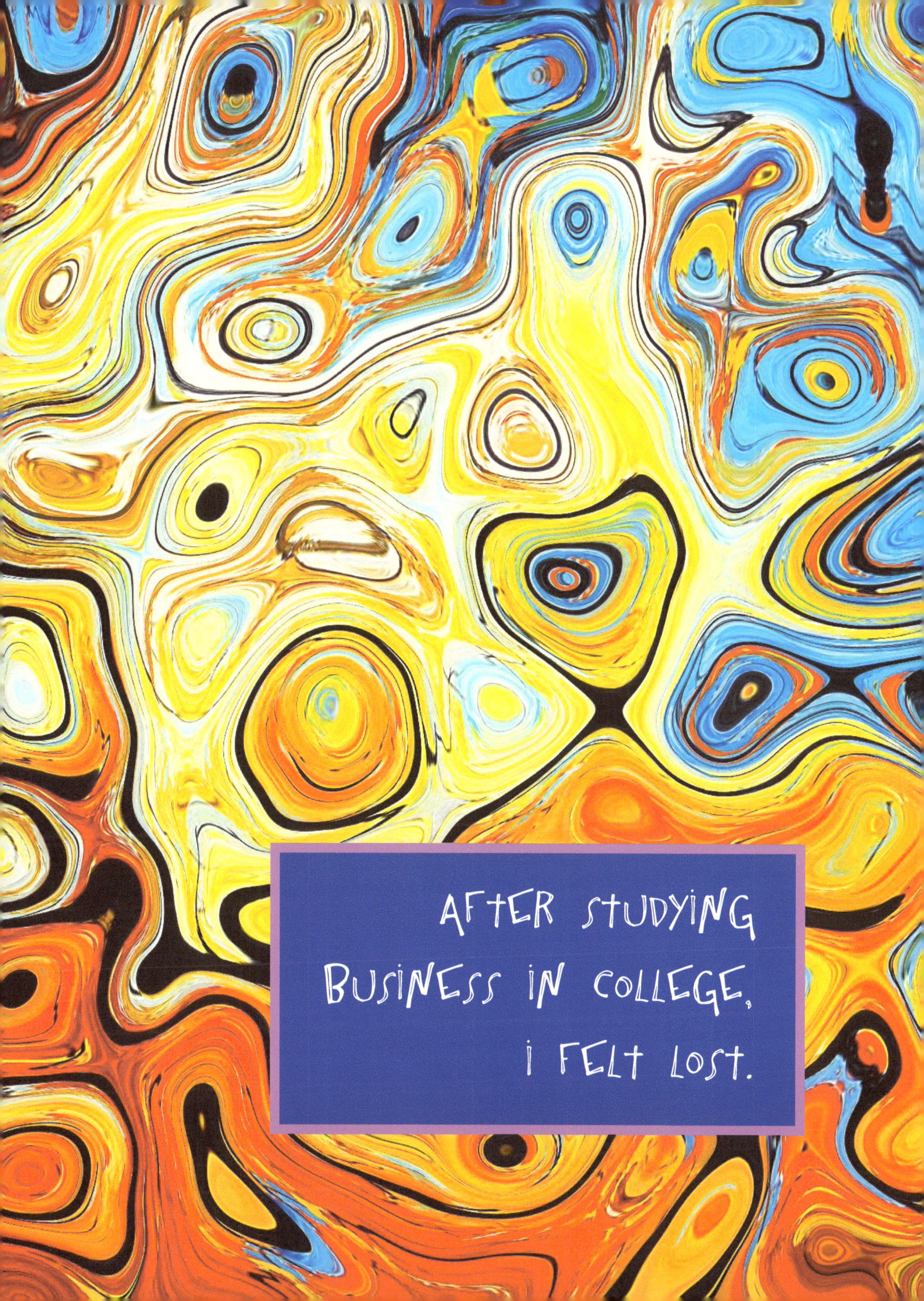

AFTER STUDYING
BUSINESS IN COLLEGE,
I FELT LOST.

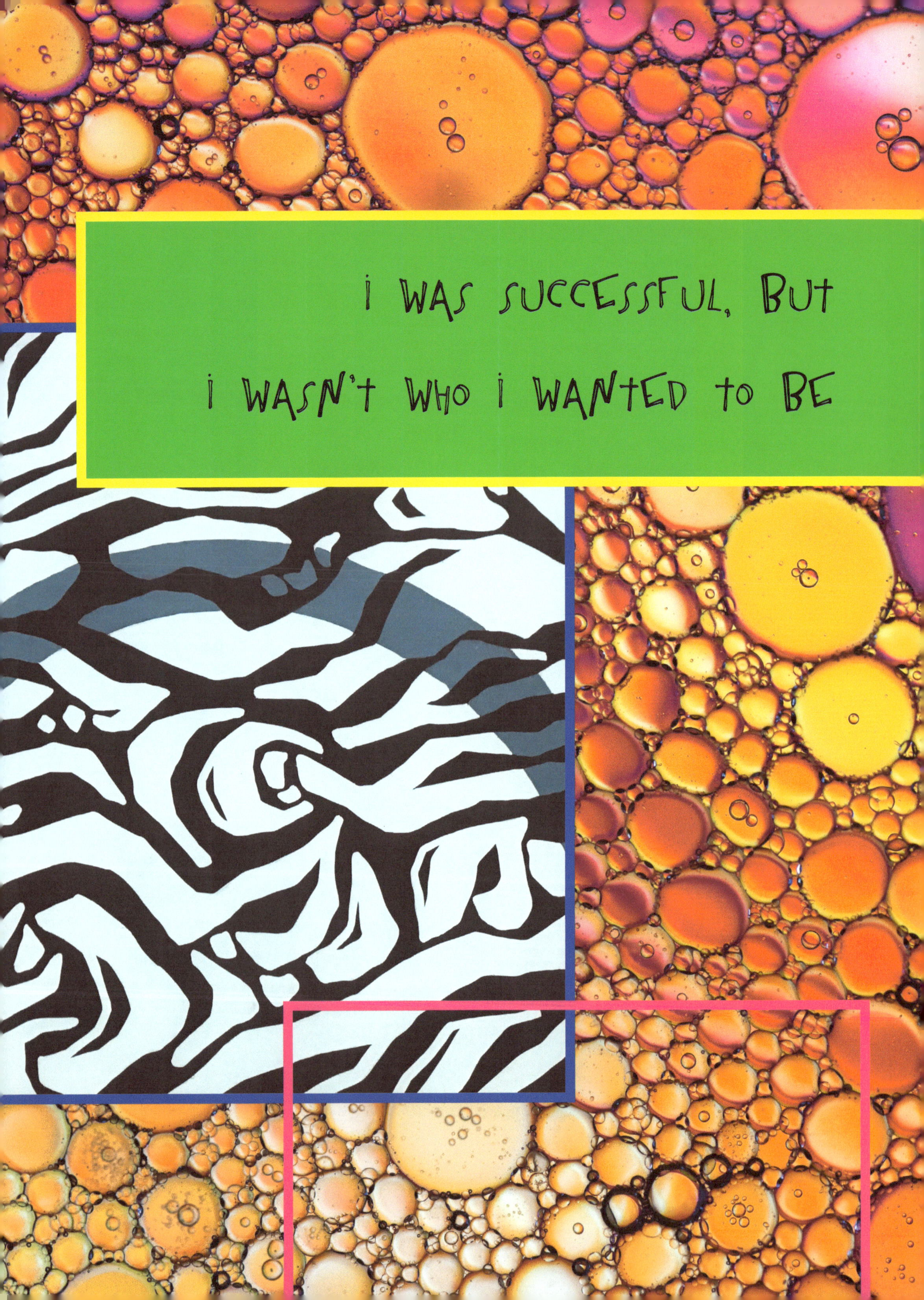

i WAS SUCCESSFUL, BUT
i WASN'T WHO i WANTED TO BE

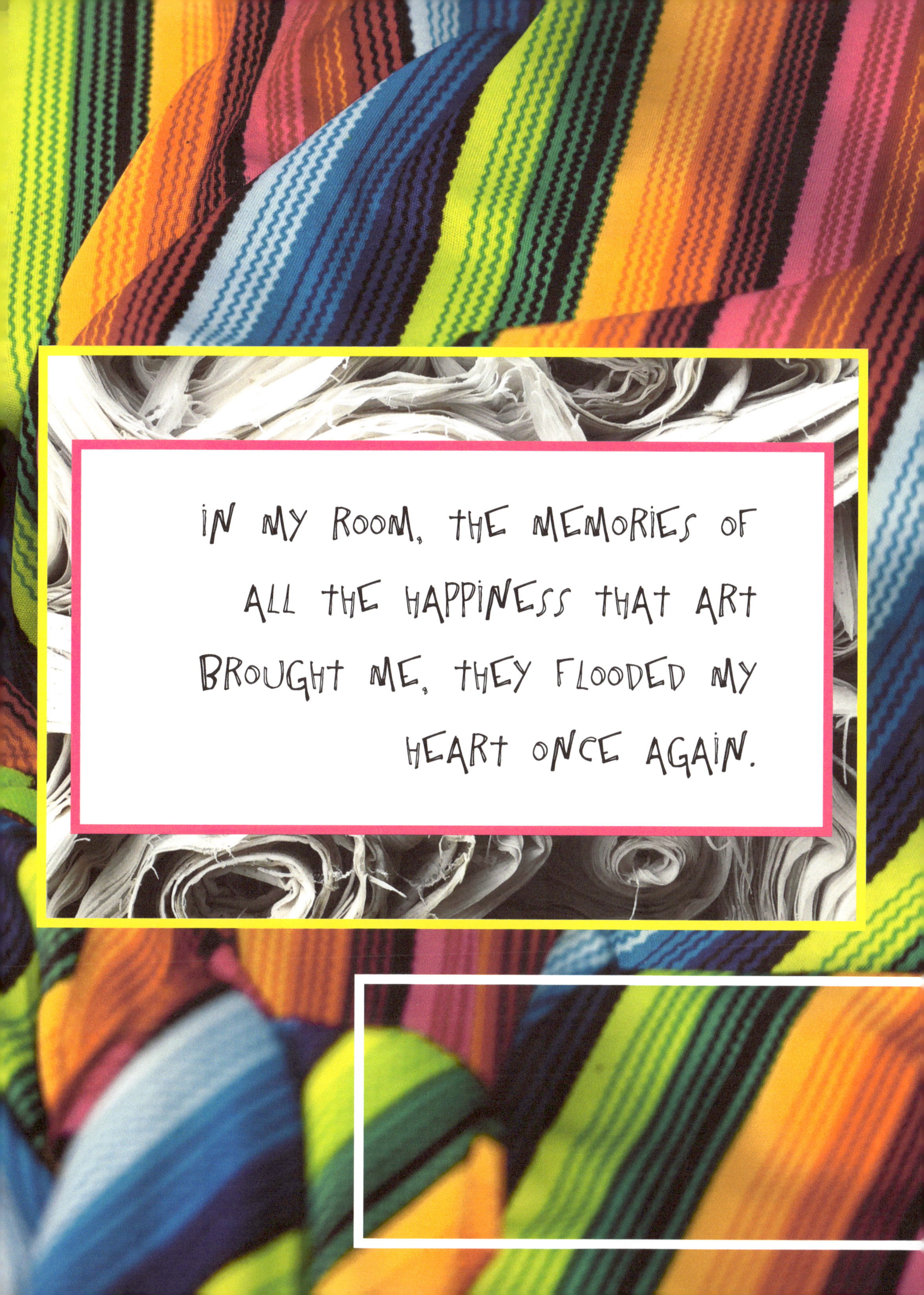
IN MY ROOM, THE MEMORIES OF
ALL THE HAPPINESS THAT ART
BROUGHT ME, THEY FLOODED MY
HEART ONCE AGAIN.

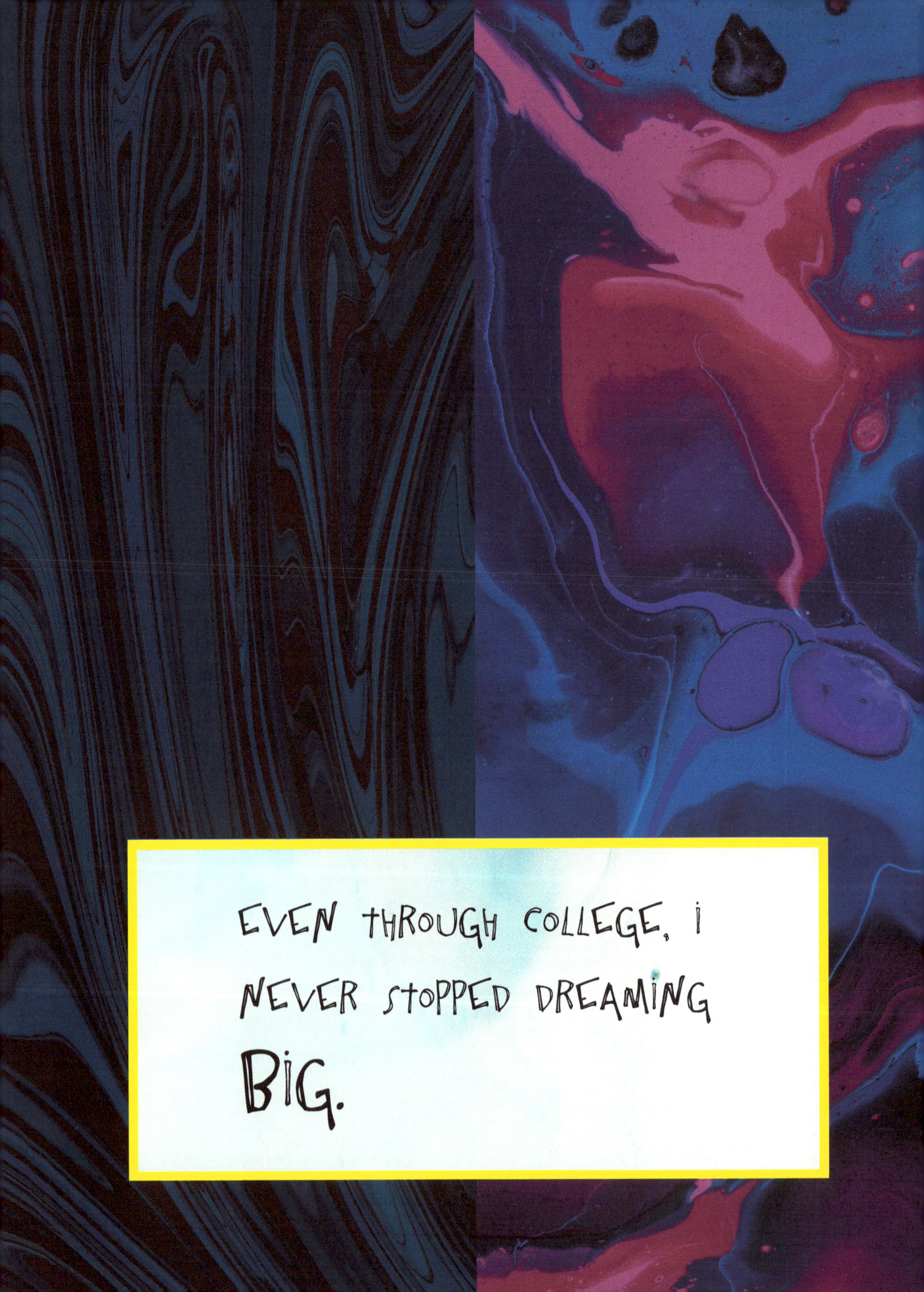

EVEN THROUGH COLLEGE, I
NEVER STOPPED DREAMING
BIG.

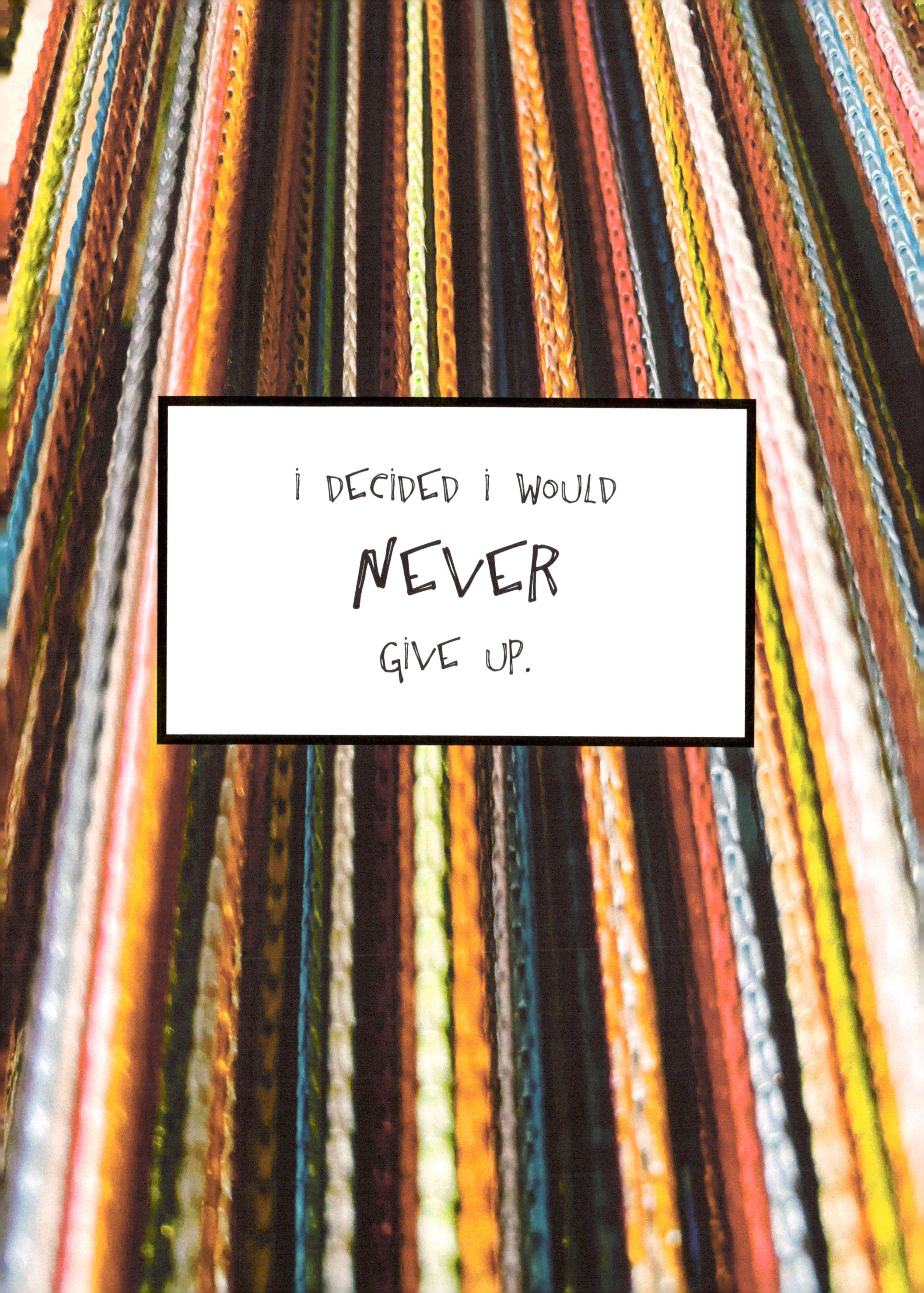

i DECiDED i WOULD
NEVER
GiVE UP.

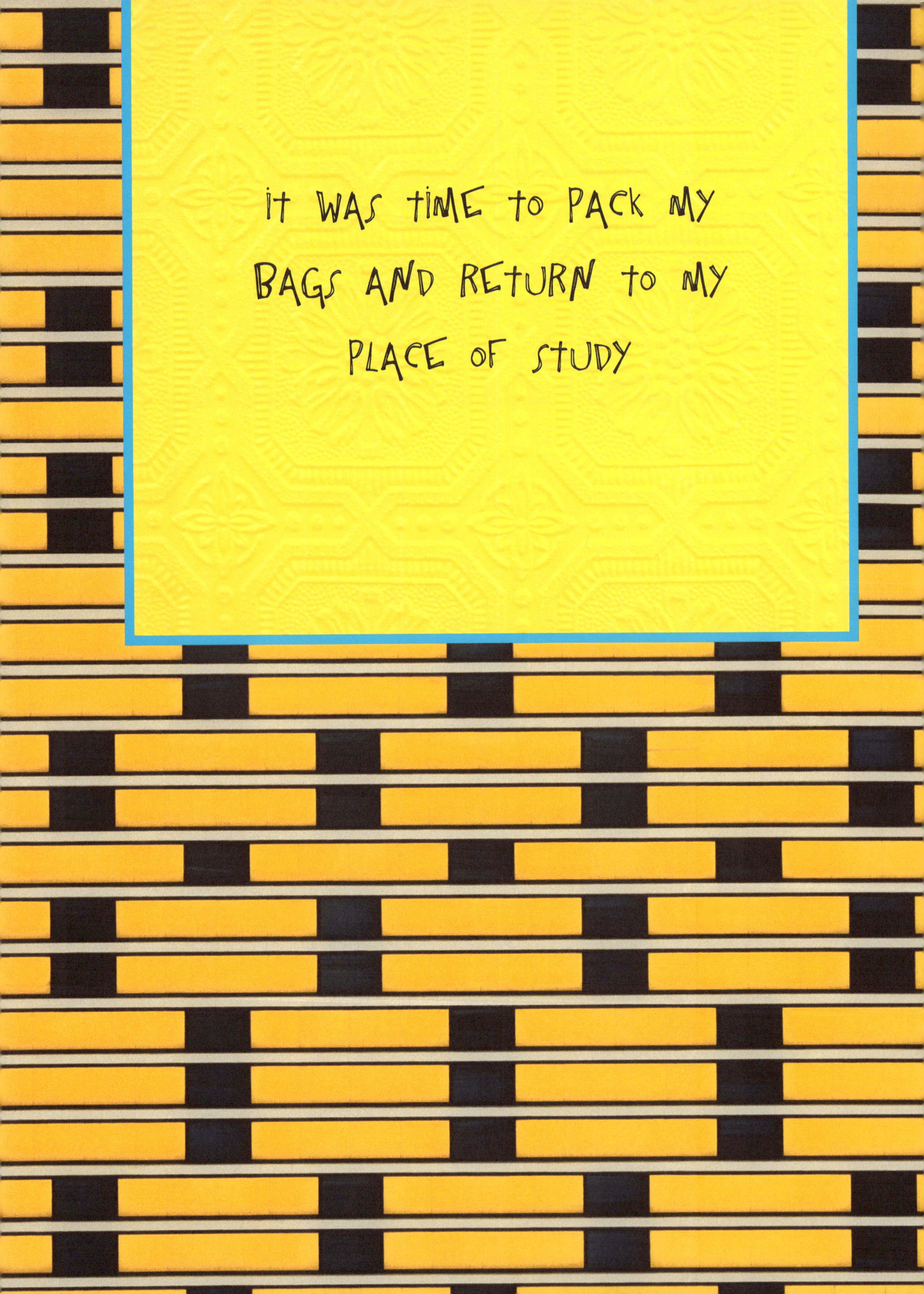

iT WAS TiME to PACK MY
BAGS AND RETURN to MY
PLACE OF STUDY

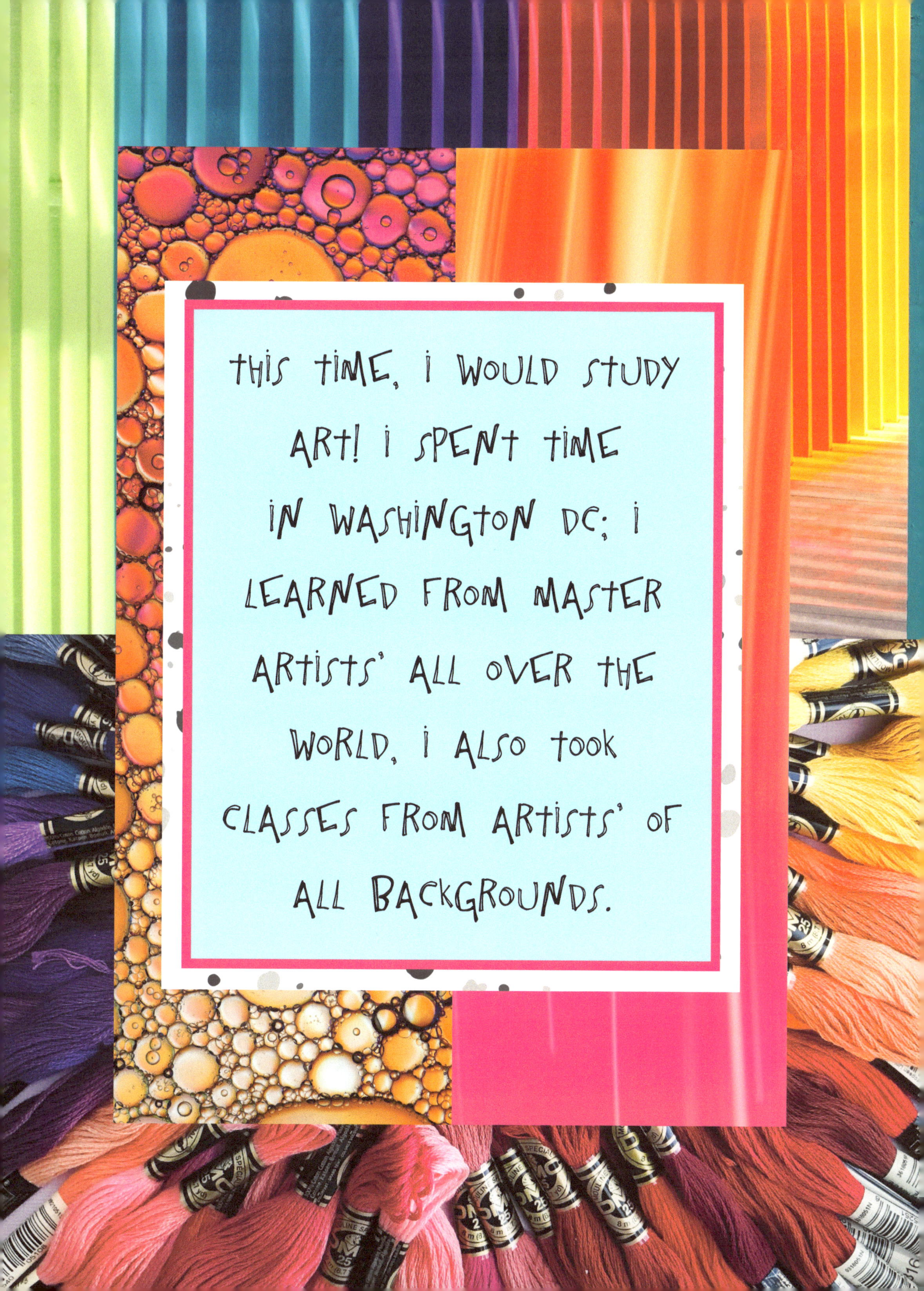
THIS TIME, I WOULD STUDY
ART! I SPENT TIME
IN WASHINGTON DC; I
LEARNED FROM MASTER
ARTISTS' ALL OVER THE
WORLD, I ALSO TOOK
CLASSES FROM ARTISTS' OF
ALL BACKGROUNDS.

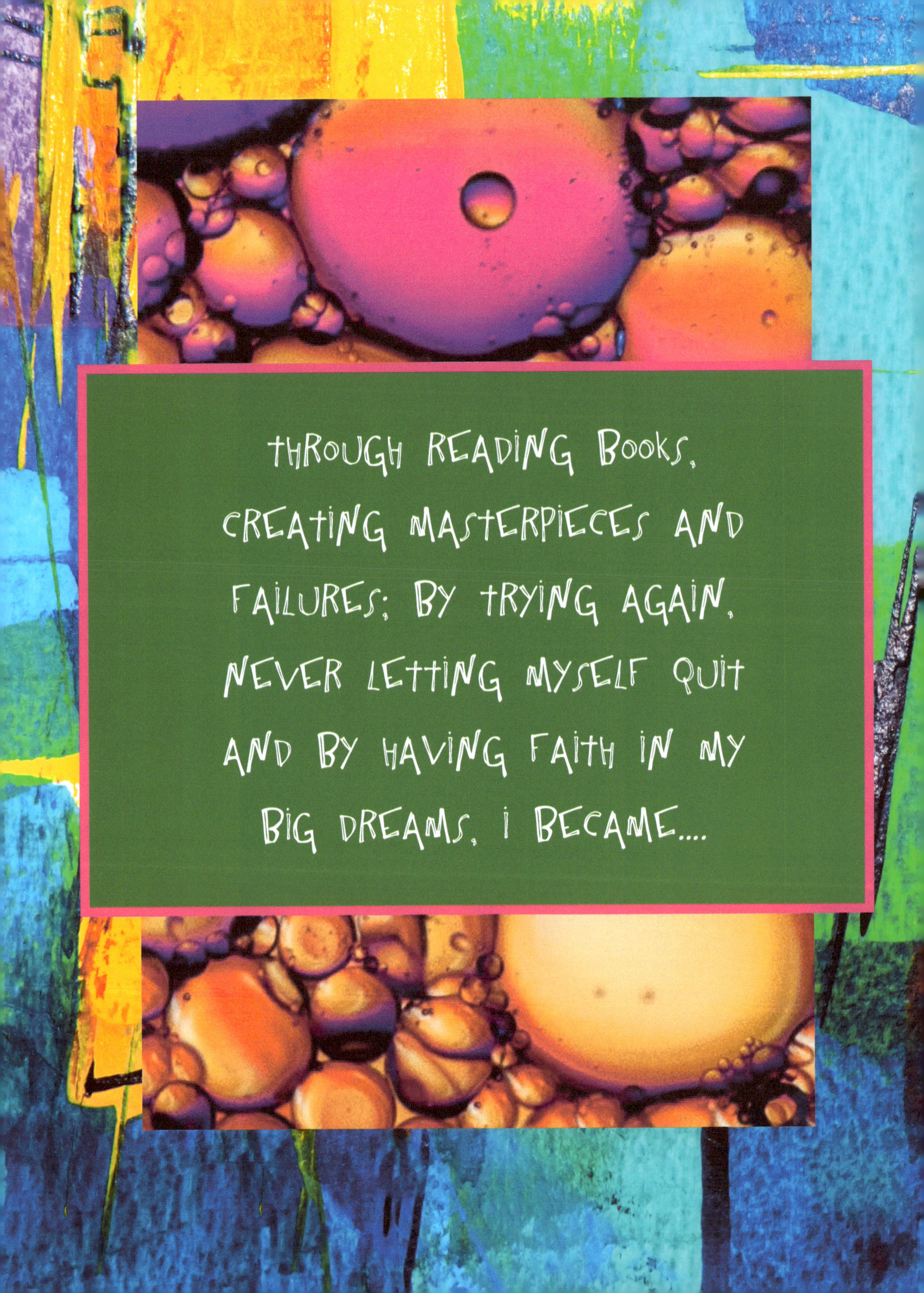

tHROUGH READiNG BOOks,
CREAtiNG MASTERPiECES AND
FAiLURES; BY tRYiNG AGAiN,
NEVER LEttiNG MYSELF QUit
AND BY HAViNG FAitH iN MY
BiG DREAMS, i BECAME....

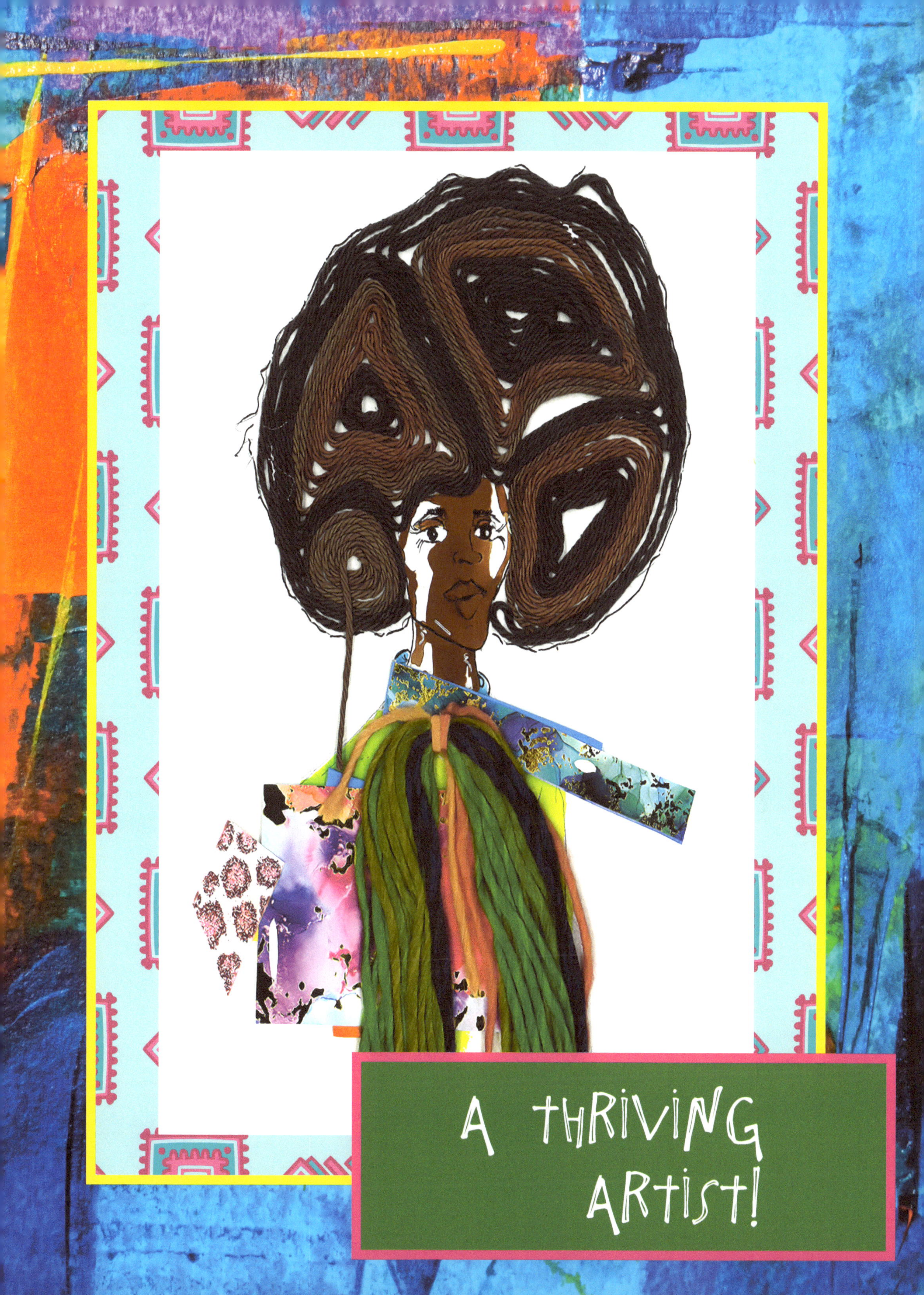
A THRIVING ARTIST!

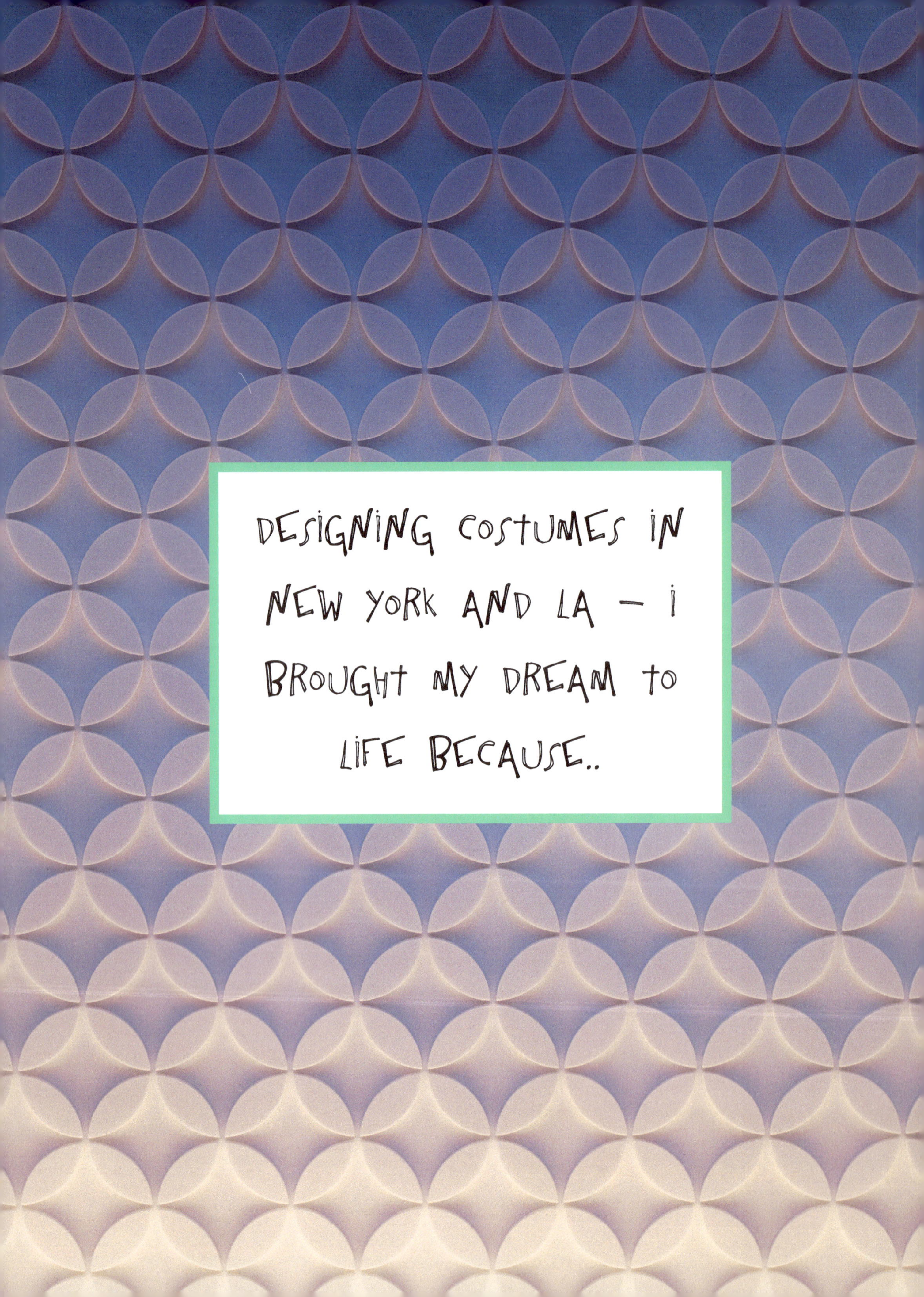

DESIGNING COSTUMES IN
NEW YORK AND LA — i
BROUGHT MY DREAM to
LIFE BECAUSE..

I AM
MY ART!

WHAT ARE YOUR
DREAMS?
WHO WILL YOU
BECOME?

to the DREAMER,
DON'T EVER GiVE UP,
YOUR FUTURE DEPENDS ON it.

to the ARTISTS WHO SEEKS
APPROVAL, LET YOUR ART SPEAK
FOR itSELF.

to the DREAMER AND ARTiST
WHO SEEKS WHAT FEELS to BE
UNOBtAiNABLE, REACH, REACH,
REACH FOR the SKY.

THEN FLY.